# Supreme Court
# Watch 2000

*Other Books by David M. O'Brien*

STORM CENTER:
THE SUPREME COURT IN AMERICAN POLITICS
FIFTH EDITION

CONSTITUTIONAL LAW AND POLITICS:
Vol. 1, STRUGGLES FOR POWER AND GOVERNMENTAL
ACCOUNTABILITY

Vol. 2, CIVIL RIGHTS AND CIVIL LIBERTIES
FOURTH EDITION

ABORTION AND AMERICAN POLITICS
(co-authored)

JUDICIAL ROULETTE

WHAT PROCESS IS DUE?
COURTS AND SCIENCE-POLICY DISPUTES

VIEWS FROM THE BENCH:
THE JUDICIARY AND CONSTITUTIONAL POLITICS
(co-authored)

THE POLITICS OF TECHNOLOGY ASSESSMENT:
INSTITUTIONS, PROCESSES, AND POLICY DISPUTES
(co-authored)

THE PUBLIC'S RIGHT TO KNOW:
THE SUPREME COURT AND THE FIRST AMENDMENT

PRIVACY, LAW, AND PUBLIC POLICY

THE POLITICS OF AMERICAN GOVERNMENT
THIRD EDITION
(co-authored)

TO DREAM OF DREAMS:
RELIGIOUS FREEDOM AND CONSTITUTIONAL POLITICS
IN POSTWAR JAPAN

JUDGES ON JUDGING

LANAHAN READINGS IN CIVIL RIGHTS AND
CIVIL LIBERTIES

# SUPREME COURT WATCH 2000

*Highlights of the 1999–2000 Term*
*Preview of the 2000–2001 Term*

## DAVID M. O'BRIEN

UNIVERSITY OF VIRGINIA

**W. W. NORTON & COMPANY**

*New York    London*

ISBN 0-393-97685-8 (pbk.)

W. W. Norton & Company, Inc., 500 Fifth Avenue, New York, N.Y. 10110
        http://www.wwnorton.com
W. W. Norton & Company Ltd., 10 Coptic Street, London WC1A 1PU

1 2 3 4 5 6 7 8 9 0

# CONTENTS

# VOLUME TWO

# PREFACE

*Supreme Court Watch 2000* examines the changes and decisions made during the Supreme Court's 1999 term. (In addition, a few of the important rulings that came down at the end of the Court's 1998 term are also included here, because it was impossible to include them in the fourth edition of *Constitutional Law and Politics*.) In addition to highlighting the major constitutional rulings in excerpts from leading cases, I discuss in section-by-section introductions other important decisions and analyze recent developments in various areas of constitutional law. The important cases that the Court has granted review and will decide in its 2000–2001 term are also previewed here. To offer even more information in an efficient format, I have included special boxes titled "The Development of Law" and "Inside the Court."

The favorable reception of and comments received on previous editions of the *Watch* have been gratifying, and I hope that this 2000 edition will further contribute to students' understanding of constitutional law, politics, and history, as well as to their appreciation for how the politics of constitutional interpretation turns on differing interpretations of constitutional politics. I am also most grateful to Robert Whiteside and to Jane Carter for doing a terrific and expeditious job of copyediting.

D.M.O.
June 28, 2000

# VOLUME ONE

# 2

---

# LAW AND POLITICS IN THE SUPREME COURT: JURISDICTION AND DECISION-MAKING PROCESS

## A. JURISDICTION AND JUSTICIABLE CONTROVERSIES

---

### THE DEVELOPMENT OF LAW

#### Other Important Rulings on Standing

| Case | Vote | Ruling |
|------|------|--------|
| *Friends of Earth, Inc. v. Laidlaw Environmental Services*, 120 S.Ct. 693 (2000) | 7:2 | In an important ruling on citizen suits brought to enforce federal environmental laws, Justice Ginsburg upheld the |

right of Friends of Earth, Inc., to sue Laidlaw Environmental Services for failing to comply with the Clean Water Act by impermissibly dumping mercury into a South Carolina river on 489 occasions from 1987 to 1995. Justice Ginsburg held that the group had shown sufficient personal injury from their loss of enjoyment of the river to gain standing to sue, without also having to prove "direct injury" to the river. The test for standing, in Justice Ginsburg's

---

words, is "not injury to the environment but injury to the plaintiff." More-over, Justice Ginsburg ruled that the fact that fines won under citizen suits go to the federal government, not to the individuals bringing the suits, does not diminish the personal injury at stake or deprive plaintiffs of standing. Joined by Justice Thomas in dissent, Justice Scalia lamented the majority's upholding of standing to bring such citizen suits and for turning "over to private citizens the function of enforcing the law."

## B. THE COURT'S DOCKET AND SCREENING CASES

The Supreme Court's docket over the last few decades has continued to grow steadily, reaching more than 8,000 cases in the 1998 term. Since the early 1990s, the largest growth has been in unpaid, or *in forma pauperis*, cases, which tend to be filed by prison inmates. (For further discussion, see Vol. 1 or 2, Ch. 2.[1]) In the 1998–1999 term, for instance, 5,689 unpaid cases were filed, compared with only 2,387 paid cases. Over the same period, the Court has steadily cut back on the number of cases granted review. As a result, the Court has been granting only around 80 to 90 cases each term, or about 1 percent of its docket.[2]

Although the Rehnquist Court gives plenary consideration to fewer cases, it has not abandoned its responsibility to supervise the lower federal courts. The Court generally takes only cases with nationwide importance, espe-cially to resolve conflicting rulings rendered by lower courts or to reverse decisions of lower federal and state courts. The Court's affirmance and reversal of lower court decisions in its 1999–2000 term is indicated on the next page.

---

[1] References to Vols. 1 and 2 are to the author's two-volume *Constitutional Law and Politics* (Norton, 4th ed., 2000).

[2] For a further discussion, see David M. O'Brien, "The Rehnquist Court's Shrinking Plenary Docket," 81 *Judicature* 58–65 (1997).

## The Court's Disposition of Appeals in the 1999 Term

|  | Affirmed | Reversed or Vacated |
|---|---|---|
| First Circuit | 1 | 0 |
| Second Circuit | 0 | 3 |
| Third Circuit | 1 | 1 |
| Fourth Circuit | 4 | 5 |
| Fifth Circuit | 4 | 6 |
| Sixth Circuit | 1 | 2 |
| Seventh Circuit | 2 | 4 |
| Eighth Circuit | 4 | 3 |
| Ninth Circuit | 1 | 9 |
| Tenth Circuit | 1 | 0 |
| Eleventh Circuit | 2 | 4 |
| Federal Circuit | 0 | 2 |
| District of Columbia Circuit | 3 | 0 |
| Other Federal Courts | 2 | 0 |
| State Courts and Other | 3 | 9 |
| *Totals | 29 | 48 |

* One decision was in a case on original jurisdiction and is not counted here.

## INSIDE THE COURT

### The Business of the Supreme Court in the 1999–2000 Term[*]

| Subject of Court Opinions | Summary | Plenary |
|---|---|---|
| Admiralty | | |
| Antitrust | | |
| Bankruptcy | | 1 |
| Bill of Rights (other than rights of accused) and Equal Protection | | 13 |
| Commerce Clause | | |
|     1. Constitutionality and construction of federal regulation | | 6 |
|     2. Constitutionality of state regulation | | 2 |
| Common Law | | |
| Miscellaneous Statutory Construction | | 11 |
| Due process | | |
|     1. Economic interests | | |
|     2. Procedure and rights of accused | 1 | 16 |
|     3. Substantive due process (noneconomic) | | 1 |
| Impairment of Contract and Just Compensation | | |
| International Law, War, and Peace | | |
| Jurisdiction, Procedure, and Practice | 2 | 14 |
| Land Legislation | | 1 |
| Native Americans | | 1 |
| Patents, Copyright, and Trademarks | | 1 |
| Other Suits Against the Government | | 3 |
| Suits by States | 1 | |
| Taxation (federal and state) | | 4 |
| Totals | 4 | 74 |

[*] Note: The classification of cases is that of the author and necessarily invites differences of opinion as to the dominant issue in some cases. Included are opinions in cases whether decided summarily or given plenary consideration, but not cases summarily disposed of by simple orders, opinions dissenting from the denial of review, and those cases that are dismissed as improvidently granted.

# H. OPINION DAYS AND COMMUNICATING DECISIONS

In April 2000 the Supreme Court began making its decisions and opinions immediately available on its Web site at http://www.supremecourtus.gov. A link to the site may also be found at the *Supreme Court Watch's* site at http://www.wwnorton.com/scww/.

---

INSIDE THE COURT

Opinion Writing during the 1999–2000 Term[*]

| Opinions | Majority | Concurring | Dissenting | Separate | Totals |
|---|---|---|---|---|---|
| Per Curiam | 5 | | | | 5 |
| Rehnquist | 9 | | 3 | 2 | 14 |
| Stevens | 7 | 7 | 16 | 3 | 33 |
| O'Connor | 9 | 6 | 1 | | 16 |
| Scalia | 8 | 7 | 8 | 2 | 25 |
| Kennedy | 9 | 5 | 4 | | 18 |
| Souter | 8 | 5 | 7 | 2 | 22 |
| Thomas | 8 | 8 | 4 | 1 | 21 |
| Ginsburg | 7 | 4 | 5 | 1 | 17 |
| Breyer | 9 | 7 | 9 | | 25 |
| Totals | 79 | 49 | 57 | 11 | 196 |

[*] Note that in *Williams v. Taylor,* Justices Stevens and O'Connor delivered opinions for the Court and, thus, there are two majority opinions in that case. Court opinions disposing of two or more companion cases are counted only once here. In addition, this table includes opinions in cases disposed of either summarily or on plenary consideration, but does not include cases summarily disposed of by simple orders or concurring or dissenting opinions from the denial of *certiorari.*

## INSIDE THE COURT

### Voting Alignments in the Rehnquist Court, 1986–1998 Terms

| | Rehnquist | White | Blackmun | Stevens | O'Connor | Scalia | Kennedy | Souter | Thomas | Brennan | Marshall | Ginsburg | Breyer |
|---|---|---|---|---|---|---|---|---|---|---|---|---|---|
| Rehnquist | -- | 80.8 | 55.2 | 52.0 | 74.2 | 78.9 | 88.9 | 69.1 | 80.0 | 47.6 | 46.4 | 65.5 | 63.0 |
| White | 80.8 | -- | 62.2 | 60.4 | 72.5 | 69.8 | 75.7 | 73.5 | 67.7 | 52.9 | 52.9 | | |
| Blackmun | 55.2 | 62.2 | -- | 72.0 | 58.4 | 49.1 | 57.6 | 64.8 | 44.4 | 77.4 | 77.0 | 68.2 | |
| Stevens | 52.0 | 60.4 | 72.0 | -- | 56.5 | 50.3 | 57.9 | 67.2 | 43.7 | 69.9 | 71.6 | 75.7 | 73.8 |
| O'Connor | 74.2 | 72.5 | 58.4 | 56.5 | -- | 72.2 | 78.7 | 72.2 | 72.2 | 49.4 | 47.9 | 66.6 | 71.9 |
| Scalia | 78.9 | 69.8 | 49.1 | 50.3 | 72.2 | -- | 76.1 | 63.1 | 87.3 | 47.5 | 45.0 | 58.1 | 54.8 |
| Kennedy | 88.9 | 75.7 | 57.6 | 57.9 | 78.7 | 76.1 | -- | 73.2 | 73.2 | 53.7 | 51.2 | 70.0 | 68.8 |
| Souter | 69.1 | 73.5 | 64.8 | 67.2 | 72.2 | 63.1 | 73.2 | -- | 59.1 | | 54.6 | 81.6 | 82.1 |
| Thomas | 80.0 | 67.7 | 44.4 | 43.7 | 72.2 | 87.3 | 73.2 | 59.1 | -- | | | 54.1 | 54.1 |
| Brennan | 47.6 | 52.9 | 77.4 | 69.9 | 49.4 | 47.5 | 53.7 | | | -- | 95.0 | | |
| Marshall | 46.4 | 52.9 | 77.0 | 71.6 | 47.9 | 45.0 | 51.2 | 54.6 | | 95.0 | -- | | |
| Ginsburg | 65.5 | | 68.2 | 75.7 | 66.6 | 58.1 | 70.0 | 81.6 | 54.1 | | | -- | 79.5 |
| Breyer | 63.0 | | | 73.8 | 71.9 | 54.8 | 68.8 | 82.1 | 54.1 | | | 79.5 | -- |

Note: The above are average percentages. The percentages for each term are from Table 1 of the *Harvard Law Review*'s annual review of the Supreme Court's term in volumes 101–13 (1988–1999).

# 4

## THE PRESIDENT AS CHIEF EXECUTIVE IN DOMESTIC AFFAIRS

### C. LEGISLATIVE POWERS IN THE ADMINISTRATIVE STATE

Reaffirming the so-called *Chevron* doctrine, set forth in *Chevron v. Natural Resources Defense Council*, 467 U.S. 837 (1984) (see Vol. 1, Ch. 4), which states that if a statute is "silent or ambiguous" on a matter, the courts will defer to the executive branch's interpretation, the Court rebuffed the U.S. Food and Drug Administration's (FDA) 1996 decision to claim jurisdiction over tobacco products. Writing for the Court in *Food and Drug Administration v. Brown and Williamson*, 120 S.Ct. 1291 (2000), Justice O'Connor held that Congress, in passing numerous laws governing tobacco products, and the FDA's own prior interpretation of its governing statute made clear Congress's intent to exempt tobacco from the FDA's jurisdiction. Moreover, Justice O'Connor observed that it was impossible for tobacco products to be rendered safe and therefore the FDA would have to ban their sale if it had jurisdiction over them. In dissent, Justice Breyer, joined by Justices Stevens, Souter, and Ginsburg, contended that the FDA could assume jurisdiction over tobacco products without having to ban their sale.

In its 2000–2001 term, the Court will consider the application of *Chevron* and the so-called nondelegation doctrine in *Browner v. American Trucking Association* (No. 99-1257). At issue is whether the Environmental Protection Agency's (EPA) revision of the Clean Air Act's provisions for national ambient air quality standards (NAAQS) on ozone was an impermissible delegation of legislative authority. The EPA is required by the Clean Air Act to periodically revise NAAQS for ozone and did so in 1997, but its new standards were immediately challenged as an exercise of unconstitutionally delegated power. The Court of Appeals for the District of Columbia Circuit agreed, concluding that the EPA construed sections of the Clean Air Act "so loosely as to render them unconstitutional delegations of legislative power."

# 6

# CONGRESS: LEGISLATIVE, TAXING, AND SPENDING POWERS

## C. FROM THE NEW DEAL CRISIS TO THE ADMINISTRATIVE STATE

In spite of recent rulings curbing congressional power under the Commerce Clause of Article I, in *United States v. Lopez*, 514 U.S. 549 (1995) (excerpted in Vol. 1, Ch. 6), and *Printz v. United States* and *Mack v. United States*, 117 S.Ct. 2365 (1997) (excerpted in Vol. 1, Ch. 7), as well as under Section 5 of the Fourteenth Amendment, in *City of Boerne v. Flores*, 521 U.S. 507 (1997) (excerpted in Vol. 2, Ch. 6), the Court unanimously upheld the Drivers' Privacy Protection Act of 1994 in *Reno v. Condon* (excerpted below). The bare majority striking down other congressional legislation, however, held firm in holding unconstitutional the Violence Against Women Act of 1994, in *United States v. Morrison* (excerpted below).

In a related ruling, *Jones v. United States*, 120 S.Ct. 2236 (2000), the Court unanimously held that a congressional statute making the offense of arson of property "used in interstate or foreign commerce" a federal crime does not extend to arson of a residential home. Writing for the Court, Justice Ginsburg emphasized that *Lopez* made clear that Congress's power over interstate commerce extends to only noncommercial activities that "significantly affect commerce" and that here, because the statute was ambiguous, it was appropriate for the Court to avoid the constitutional question of whether Congress aimed to reach the arson of homes, which is a paradigmatic common-law state crime, and thereby alter the federal-state balance in the prosecution of crime.

In its 2000–2001 term, the Court will consider whether the assertion of jurisdiction over intrastate waters by the U.S. Army Corps of Engineers to preserve the habitat of migratory birds is within its powers under the Clean Water Act and congressional regulatory powers under the Commerce Clause.

A group of municipalities sought to expand their waste disposal facilities, but the U.S. Army Corps required them to obtain a permit and invoked the Clean Water Act as authority for that requirement. The Court of Appeals for the Seventh Circuit upheld the U.S. Army Corps' jurisdiction and congressional power over such matters on the ground that the purpose of the Clean Water Act included the restoration of "the biological integrity of the Nation's waters" and that the destruction of migratory-bird habitat "substantially affects" interstate commerce (191 F.3d 845 [1999]). That decision was appealed, and the Supreme Court granted review in *Solid Waste Agency v. U.S. Army Corps of Engineers* (No. 99-1178).

## *Reno v. Condon*
### 120 S.Ct. 666 (2000)

Congress enacted the Drivers' Privacy Protection Act of 1994 to protect individuals' privacy and other interests. The law regulates the disclosure of personal information contained in the records of state motor vehicle departments. Specifically, it forbids the disclosure of personal information—name, address, telephone number, identification number, photograph, and medical information—except for certain purposes related, for instance, to driver safety and motor vehicle recalls. The law also regulates the resale of such information by private parties and imposes penalties for violations. South Carolina and some other states regularly sold such information and immediately challenged the constitutionality of the law. Charlie Condon, South Carolina's attorney general, argued that the law violated the Tenth and Eleventh Amendments and was incompatible with principles of federalism. A federal district court agreed and was affirmed by the Court of Appeals for the Fourth Circuit. Attorney General Janet Reno appealed and the Supreme Court granted review.

The appellate court's decision was reversed in a unanimous opinion for the Court delivered by Chief Justice Rehnquist.

Chief Justice REHNQUIST delivered the opinion of the Court.

The Driver's Privacy Protection Act of 1994 (DPPA or Act) regulates the disclosure of personal information contained in the records of state motor vehicle departments (DMVs). We hold that in enacting this statute Congress did not run afoul of the federalism principles enunciated in *New York v. United States*, 505 U.S. 144 (1992), and *Printz v. United States*, 521 U.S. 898 (1997). . . .

The United States asserts that the DPPA is a proper exercise of Congress' authority to regulate interstate commerce under the Commerce Clause. The United

States bases its Commerce Clause argument on the fact that the personal, identifying information that the DPPA regulates is a "thin[g] in interstate commerce," and that the sale or release of that information in interstate commerce is therefore a proper subject of congressional regulation. *United States v. Lopez,* 514 U.S. 549 (1995). We agree with the United States' contention. The motor vehicle information which the States have historically sold is used by insurers, manufacturers, direct marketers, and others engaged in interstate commerce to contact drivers with customized solicitations. The information is also used in the stream of interstate commerce by various public and private entities for matters related to interstate motoring. Because drivers' information is, in this context, an article of commerce, its sale or release into the interstate stream of business is sufficient to support congressional regulation. We therefore need not address the Government's alternative argument that the States' individual, intrastate activities in gathering, maintaining, and distributing drivers' personal information has a sufficiently substantial impact on interstate commerce to create a constitutional base for federal legislation.

But the fact that drivers' personal information is, in the context of this case, an article in interstate commerce does not conclusively resolve the constitutionality of the DPPA. In *New York* and *Printz,* we held federal statutes invalid, not because Congress lacked legislative authority over the subject matter, but because those statutes violated the principles of federalism contained in the Tenth Amendment. . . .

We agree with South Carolina's assertion that the DPPA's provisions will require time and effort on the part of state employees, but reject the State's argument that the DPPA violates the principles laid down in either *New York* or *Printz.* We think, instead, that this case is governed by our decision in *South Carolina v. Baker,* 485 U.S. 505 (1988). In *Baker,* we upheld a statute that prohibited States from issuing unregistered bonds because the law "regulate[d] state activities," rather than "seek[ing] to control or influence the manner in which States regulate private parties." We further noted: "The NGA [National Governor's Association] nonetheless contends that Section 310 has commandeered the state legislative and administrative process because many state legislatures had to amend a substantial number of statutes in order to issue bonds in registered form and because state officials had to devote substantial effort to determine how best to implement a registered bond system. Such 'commandeering' is, however, an inevitable consequence of regulating a state activity. Any federal regulation demands compliance. That a State wishing to engage in certain activity must take administrative and sometimes legislative action to comply with federal standards regulating that activity is a commonplace that presents no constitutional defect."

Like the statute at issue in *Baker,* the DPPA does not require the States in their sovereign capacity to regulate their own citizens. The DPPA regulates the States as the owners of databases. It does not require the South Carolina Legislature to enact any laws or regulations, and it does not require state officials to assist in the enforcement of federal statutes regulating private individuals. We accordingly conclude that the DPPA is consistent with the constitutional principles enunciated in *New York* and *Printz.* . . .

The judgment of the Court of Appeals is therefore reversed.

# United States v. Morrison
## 120 S.Ct. 1740 (2000)

After holding extensive hearings on gender-motivated violence and find-ing that such violence costs the national economy $3 billion annually, Con-gress enacted the Violence Against Women Act of 1994, which made violence against women a federal crime and, in Section 13981 of the U.S. Code, created as a remedy a private cause of action for victims to sue their attackers for damages. In 1994, Christy Brozonkala, a first-year student at Virginia Polytechnic Institute and State University, was allegedly raped in her dormitory room by two football players, Antonio Morrison and James Crawford. No criminal charges were filed against the latter, but subse-quently Brozonkala sued them for damages under the Violence Against Women Act. A federal district court, however, concluded that the law was an unconstitutional intrusion on traditional state concerns, and the Court of Appeals for the Fourth Circuit agreed, relying on *United States v. Lopez*, 514 U.S. 549 (1995), and *City of Boerne v. Flores*, 521 U.S. 507 (1997). The U.S. government and Brozonkala appealed, and 36 states joined a brief in support of the law. The Supreme Court granted review.

The decision of the appellate court was affirmed by a five to four vote. Chief Justice Rehnquist delivered the opinion for the Court. Justice Thomas filed a concurring opinion. Justices Souter and Breyer filed dissenting opinions, which were joined by Justices Ginsburg and Stevens.

Chief Justice REHNQUIST delivered the opinion of the Court.

The United States Court of Appeals for the Fourth Circuit, sitting *en banc*, struck down Section 13981 because it concluded that Congress lacked consti-tutional authority to enact the section's civil remedy. Believing that these cases are controlled by our decisions in *United States v. Lopez*, 514 U.S. 549 (1995), *United States v. Harris*, 106 U.S. 629 (1883), and the *Civil Rights Cases*, 109 U.S. 3 (1883), we affirm. . . .

Every law enacted by Congress must be based on one or more of its powers enumerated in the Constitution. Congress explicitly identified the sources of fed-eral authority on which it relied in enacting Section 13981. It said that a "federal civil rights cause of action" is established "[p]ursuant to the affirmative power of Congress under section 5 of the Fourteenth Amendment to the Constitution, as well as under section 8 of Article I of the Constitution." We address Congress' authority to enact this remedy under each of these constitutional provisions in turn. . . .

As we discussed at length in *Lopez*, our interpretation of the Commerce Clause has changed as our Nation has developed. We need not repeat that detailed review of the Commerce Clause's history here; it suffices to say that, in the years since *NLRB v. Jones & Laughlin Steel Corp.*, 301 U.S. 1 (1937), Congress has had considerably greater latitude in regulating conduct and transactions under the Commerce Clause than our previous case law permitted.

As we observed in *Lopez,* modern Commerce Clause jurisprudence has "identified three broad categories of activity that Congress may regulate under its commerce power." "First, Congress may regulate the use of the channels of interstate commerce" (citing *Heart of Atlanta Motel, Inc. v. United States*, 379 U.S. 241, 256 [1964]; *United States v. Darby*, 312 U.S. 100 [1941]). "Second, Congress is empowered to regulate and protect the instrumentalities of interstate commerce, or persons or things in interstate commerce, even though the threat may come only from intrastate activities" (citing *Shreveport Rate Cases*, 234 U.S. 342 [1914]; *Southern R. Co. v. United States*, 222 U.S. 20 [1911]; *Perez* [*v. United States*, 402 U.S. 146 (1971)]). "Finally, Congress' commerce authority includes the power to regulate those activities having a substantial relation to interstate commerce, i.e., those activities that substantially affect interstate commerce" (citing *Jones & Laughlin Steel*).

Petitioners do not contend that these cases fall within either of the first two of these categories of Commerce Clause regulation. They seek to sustain Section 13981 as a regulation of activity that substantially affects interstate commerce. Given Section 13981's focus on gender-motivated violence wherever it occurs (rather than violence directed at the instrumentalities of interstate commerce, interstate markets, or things or persons in interstate commerce), we agree that this is the proper inquiry.

Since *Lopez* most recently canvassed and clarified our case law governing this third category of Commerce Clause regulation, it provides the proper framework for conducting the required analysis of Section 13981. In *Lopez,* we held that the Gun-Free School Zones Act of 1990, 18 U.S.C. Section 922(q)(1)(A), which made it a federal crime to knowingly possess a firearm in a school zone, exceeded Congress' authority under the Commerce Clause. Several significant considerations contributed to our decision.

First, . . . "Where economic activity substantially affects interstate commerce, legislation regulating that activity will be sustained." . . .

The second consideration that we found important . . . was that the statute contained "no express jurisdictional element which might limit its reach to a discrete set of firearm possessions that additionally have an explicit connection with or effect on interstate commerce." Such a jurisdictional element may establish that the enactment is in pursuance of Congress' regulation of interstate commerce.

Third, we noted that neither Section 922(q) "nor its legislative history contain[s] express congressional findings regarding the effects upon interstate commerce of gun possession in a school zone." While "Congress normally is not required to make formal findings as to the substantial burdens that an activity has on interstate commerce," the existence of such findings may "enable us to evaluate the legislative judgment that the activity in question substantially affect[s] interstate commerce, even though no such substantial effect [is] visible to the naked eye."

Finally, our decision in *Lopez* rested in part on the fact that the link between gun possession and a substantial effect on interstate commerce was attenuated. . . . We rejected these "costs of crime" and "national productivity" arguments because they would permit Congress to "regulate not only all violent crime, but all activities that might lead to violent crime, regardless of how tenuously they relate to interstate commerce."

With these principles underlying our Commerce Clause jurisprudence as reference points, the proper resolution of the present cases is clear. Gender-motivated crimes of violence are not, in any sense of the phrase, economic activity. While we need not adopt a categorical rule against aggregating the effects of any non-economic activity in order to decide these cases, thus far in our Nation's history our cases have upheld Commerce Clause regulation of intrastate activity only where that activity is economic in nature.

Like the Gun-Free School Zones Act at issue in *Lopez*, Section 13981 contains no jurisdictional element establishing that the federal cause of action is in pursuance of Congress' power to regulate interstate commerce. Although *Lopez* makes clear that such a jurisdictional element would lend support to the argument that Section 13981 is sufficiently tied to interstate commerce, Congress elected to cast Section 13981's remedy over a wider, and more purely intrastate, body of violent crime.

In contrast with the lack of congressional findings that we faced in *Lopez*, Section 13981 is supported by numerous findings regarding the serious impact that gender-motivated violence has on victims and their families. But the existence of congressional findings is not sufficient, by itself, to sustain the constitutionality of Commerce Clause legislation. As we stated in *Lopez*, "[S]imply because Congress may conclude that a particular activity substantially affects interstate commerce does not necessarily make it so." Rather, "[w]hether particular operations affect interstate commerce sufficiently to come under the constitutional power of Congress to regulate them is ultimately a judicial rather than a legislative question, and can be settled finally only by this Court."

In these cases, Congress' findings are substantially weakened by the fact that they rely so heavily on a method of reasoning that we have already rejected as unworkable if we are to maintain the Constitution's enumeration of powers. Congress found that gender-motivated violence affects interstate commerce "by deterring potential victims from traveling interstate, from engaging in employment in interstate business, and from transacting with business, and in places involved in interstate commerce; by diminishing national productivity, increasing medical and other costs, and decreasing the supply of and the demand for interstate products." Given these findings and petitioners' arguments, the concern that we expressed in *Lopez* that Congress might use the Commerce Clause to completely obliterate the Constitution's distinction between national and local authority seems well founded. . . . If accepted, petitioners' reasoning would allow Congress to regulate any crime as long as the nationwide, aggregated impact of that crime has substantial effects on employment, production, transit, or consumption. Indeed, if Congress may regulate gender-motivated violence, it would be able to regulate murder or any other type of violence since gender-motivated violence, as a subset of all violent crime, is certain to have lesser economic impacts than the larger class of which it is a part. . . .

We accordingly reject the argument that Congress may regulate noneconomic, violent criminal conduct based solely on that conduct's aggregate effect on interstate commerce. The Constitution requires a distinction between what is truly national and what is truly local. In recognizing this fact we preserve one of the few principles that has been consistent since the Clause was adopted. The regulation and punishment of intrastate violence that is not directed at the instrumentalities, channels, or goods involved in interstate commerce has always been the province of the States.

Because we conclude that the Commerce Clause does not provide Congress with authority to enact Section 13981, we address petitioners' alternative argument that the section's civil remedy should be upheld as an exercise of Congress' remedial power under Section 5 of the Fourteenth Amendment.

The principles governing an analysis of congressional legislation under Section 5 are well settled. . . . *City of Boerne v. Flores*, 521 U.S. 507 (1997). Section 5 is "a positive grant of legislative power," *Katzenbach v. Morgan*, 384 U.S. 641 (1966), that includes authority to "prohibit conduct which is not itself unconstitutional and [to] intrud[e] into 'legislative spheres of autonomy previously reserved to the States.'" However, "[a]s broad as the congressional enforcement power is, it is not unlimited." *Oregon v. Mitchell*, 400 U.S. 112 (1970). . . .

As our cases have established, state-sponsored gender discrimination violates equal protection unless it "serves important governmental objectives and the discriminatory means employed" are "substantially related to the achievement of those objectives." *United States v. Virginia*, 518 U.S. 515 (1996). However, the language and purpose of the Fourteenth Amendment place certain limitations on the manner in which Congress may attack discriminatory conduct. These limitations are necessary to prevent the Fourteenth Amendment from obliterating the Framers' carefully crafted balance of power between the States and the National Government. Foremost among these limitations is the time-honored principle that the Fourteenth Amendment, by its very terms, prohibits only state action.

Shortly after the Fourteenth Amendment was adopted, we decided two cases interpreting the Amendment's provisions, *United States v. Harris*, 106 U.S. 629 (1883), and the *Civil Rights Cases*, 109 U.S. 3 (1883). In *Harris*, the Court considered a challenge to Section 2 of the Civil Rights Act of 1871. That section sought to punish "private persons" for "conspiring to deprive any one of the equal protection of the laws enacted by the State." We concluded that this law exceeded Congress' Section 5 power because the law was "directed exclusively against the action of private persons, without reference to the laws of the State, or their administration by her officers."

We reached a similar conclusion in the *Civil Rights Cases*. In those consolidated cases, we held that the public accommodation provisions of the Civil Rights Act of 1875, which applied to purely private conduct, were beyond the scope of the Section 5 enforcement power. . . .

Petitioners alternatively argue that, unlike the situation in the *Civil Rights Cases*, here there has been gender-based disparate treatment by state authorities, whereas in those cases there was no indication of such state action. There is abundant evidence, however, to show that the Congresses that enacted the Civil Rights Acts of 1871 and 1875 had a purpose similar to that of Congress in enacting Section 13981: There were state laws on the books bespeaking equality of treatment, but in the administration of these laws there was discrimination against newly freed slaves. . . .

But even if that distinction were valid, we do not believe it would save Section 13981's civil remedy. For the remedy is simply not "corrective in its character, adapted to counteract and redress the operation of such prohibited [s]tate laws or proceedings of [s]tate officers." *Civil Rights Cases*. Or, as we have phrased it in more recent cases, prophylactic legislation under Section 5 must have a "congruence and proportionality between the injury to be prevented or remedied and the means adopted to that end." *Florida Prepaid Postsecondary Ed. Expense Bd. v. College Savings Bank*, 527 U.S. 627 (1999); *Flores*. Section 13981 is not aimed at proscribing discrimination by officials which the Fourteenth Amendment might not itself proscribe; it is directed not at any State or state actor, but at individuals who have committed criminal acts motivated by gender bias. . . .

[Section 13981] is, therefore, unlike any of the Section 5 remedies that we have previously upheld. For example, in *Katzenbach v. Morgan*, 384 U.S. 641 (1966), Congress prohibited New York from imposing literacy tests as a prerequisite for voting because it found that such a requirement disenfranchised thousands of Puerto Rican immigrants who had been educated in the Spanish language of their home territory. That law, which we upheld, was directed at New York officials who administered the State's election law and prohibited them from using a provision of that law. In *South Carolina v. Katzenbach*, 383 U.S. 301 (1966), Congress imposed voting rights requirements on States that, Congress found, had a history of discriminating against blacks in voting. The remedy was also directed at state officials in those States. . . .

For these reasons, we conclude that Congress' power under Section 5 does not extend to the enactment of Section 13981.


Justice THOMAS, concurring.

The majority opinion correctly applies our decision in *United States v. Lopez* and I join it in full. I write separately only to express my view that the very notion of a "substantial effects" test under the Commerce Clause is inconsistent with the original understanding of Congress' powers and with this Court's early Commerce Clause cases. By continuing to apply this rootless and malleable standard, however circumscribed, the Court has encouraged the Federal Government to persist in its view that the Commerce Clause has virtually no limits. Until this Court replaces its existing Commerce Clause jurisprudence with a standard more consistent with the original understanding, we will continue to see Congress appropriating state police powers under the guise of regulating commerce.


Justice SOUTER, with whom Justice STEVENS, Justice GINSBURG, and Justice BREYER join, dissenting.

Congress has the power to legislate with regard to activity that, in the aggregate, has a substantial effect on interstate commerce. See *Wickard v. Filburn*, 317 U.S. 111 (1942). The fact of such a substantial effect is not an issue for the courts in the first instance, but for the Congress, whose institutional capacity for gathering evidence and taking testimony far exceeds ours. By passing legislation, Congress indicates its conclusion, whether explicitly or not, that facts support its exercise of the commerce power. The business of the courts is to review the congressional assessment, not for soundness but simply for the rationality of concluding that a jurisdictional basis exists in fact. Any explicit findings that Congress chooses to make, though not dispositive of the question of rationality, may advance judicial review by identifying factual authority on which Congress relied.

One obvious difference from *United States v. Lopez* is the mountain of data assembled by Congress here showing the effects of violence against women on interstate commerce. Passage of the Act in 1994 was preceded by four years of hearings, which included testimony from physicians and law professors; from survivors of rape and domestic violence; and from representatives of state law enforcement and private business. The record includes reports on gender bias from task forces in 21 States, and we have the benefit of specific factual findings in the eight separate Reports issued by Congress and its committees over the long course leading to enactment.

With respect to domestic violence, Congress received evidence for the following findings: "Three out of four American women will be victims of violent crimes sometime during their life." "Violence is the leading cause of injuries to women ages 15 to 44." "[A]s many as 50 percent of homeless women and children are fleeing domestic violence." "Since 1974, the assault rate against women has outstripped the rate for men by at least twice for some age groups and far more for others." "[B]attering is the single largest cause of injury to women in the United States." "An estimated 4 million American women are battered each year by their husbands or partners." "Over 1 million women in the United States seek medical assistance each year for injuries sustained [from] their husbands or other partners." "Between 2,000 and 4,000 women die every year from [domestic] abuse." "Partial estimates show that violent crime against women costs this country at least 3 billion—not million, but billion—dollars a year." "[E]stimate[s] suggest that we spend $5 to $10 billion a year on health care, criminal justice, and other social costs of domestic violence."

The evidence as to rape was similarly extensive, supporting these conclusions: "[The incidence of] rape rose four times as fast as the total national crime rate over the past 10 years." "According to one study, close to half a million girls now in high school will be raped before they graduate." "[One hundred twenty-five thousand] college women can expect to be raped during this—or any—year." "[T]hree-quarters of women never go to the movies alone after dark because of the fear of rape and nearly 50 percent do not use public transit alone after dark for the same reason." "[Forty-one] percent of judges surveyed believed that juries give sexual assault victims less credibility than other crime victims." "Less than 1 percent of all [rape] victims have collected damages." "[A]n individual who commits rape has only about 4 chances in 100 of being arrested, prosecuted, and found guilty of any offense." "Almost one-quarter of convicted rapists never go to prison and another quarter received sentences in local jails where the average sentence is 11 months." "[A]lmost 50 percent of rape victims lose their jobs or are forced to quit because of the crime's severity."

Based on the data thus partially summarized, Congress found that "crimes of violence motivated by gender have a substantial adverse effect on interstate commerce, by deterring potential victims from traveling interstate, from engaging in employment in interstate business, and from transacting with business, and in places involved in interstate commerce[,] 'by diminishing national productivity, increasing medical and other costs, and decreasing the supply of and the demand for interstate products.'"

Congress thereby explicitly stated the predicate for the exercise of its Commerce Clause power. Is its conclusion irrational in view of the data amassed? True, the methodology of particular studies may be challenged, and some of the figures arrived at may be disputed. But the sufficiency of the evidence before Congress to provide a rational basis for the finding cannot seriously be questioned.

Indeed, the legislative record here is far more voluminous than the record compiled by Congress and found sufficient in two prior cases upholding Title II of the Civil Rights Act of 1964 against Commerce Clause challenges. In *Heart of Atlanta Motel, Inc. v. United States*, 379 U.S. 241 (1964), and *Katzenbach v. McClung*, 379 U.S. 294 (1964), the Court referred to evidence showing the consequences of racial discrimination by motels and restaurants on interstate commerce. Congress had relied on compelling anecdotal reports that individual instances of segregation cost thousands to millions of dollars.

While Congress did not, to my knowledge, calculate aggregate dollar values for the nationwide effects of racial discrimination in 1964, in 1994 it did rely on evidence of the harms caused by domestic violence and sexual assault, citing annual costs of $3 billion in 1990, and $5 to $10 billion in 1993. Equally important, though, gender-based violence in the 1990's was shown to operate in a manner similar to racial discrimination in the 1960's in reducing the mobility of employees and their production and consumption of goods shipped in interstate commerce. Like racial discrimination, "[g]ender-based violence bars its most likely targets—women—from full partic[ipation] in the national economy."

If the analogy to the Civil Rights Act of 1964 is not plain enough, one can always look back a bit further. In *Wickard*, we upheld the application of the Agricultural Adjustment Act to the planting and consumption of homegrown wheat. The effect on interstate commerce in that case followed from the possibility that wheat grown at home for personal consumption could either be drawn into the market by rising prices, or relieve its grower of any need to purchase wheat in the market. The Commerce Clause predicate was simply the effect of the production of wheat for home consumption on supply and demand in interstate commerce. Supply and demand for goods in interstate commerce will also be affected by the deaths of 2,000 to 4,000 women annually at the hands of domestic abusers, and by the reduction in the work force by the 100,000 or more rape victims who lose their jobs each year or are forced to quit. Violence against women may be found to affect interstate commerce and affect it substantially.

The Act would have passed muster at any time between *Wickard* in 1942 and *Lopez* in 1995, a period in which the law enjoyed a stable understanding that congressional power under the Commerce Clause, complemented by the authority of the Necessary and Proper Clause, Art. I. Sec. 8, cl. 18, extended to all activity that, when aggregated, has a substantial effect on interstate commerce. As already noted, this understanding was secure even against the turmoil at the passage of the Civil Rights Act of 1964, in the aftermath of which the Court not only reaffirmed the cumulative effects and rational basis features of the substantial effects test, see *Heart of Atlanta, McClung*, but declined to limit the commerce power through a formal distinction between legislation focused on "commerce" and statutes addressing "moral and social wrong[s]."

The fact that the Act does not pass muster before the Court today is therefore proof, to a degree that *Lopez* was not, that the Court's nominal adherence to the substantial effects test is merely that. Although a new jurisprudence has not emerged with any distinctness, it is clear that some congressional conclusions about obviously substantial, cumulative effects on commerce are being assigned lesser values than the once-stable doctrine would assign them. These devaluations are accomplished not by any express repudiation of the substantial effects test or its application through the aggregation of individual conduct, but by supplanting rational basis scrutiny with a new criterion of review.

Thus the elusive heart of the majority's analysis in these cases is its statement that Congress's findings of fact are "weakened" by the presence of a disfavored "method of reasoning." This seems to suggest that the "substantial effects" analysis is not a factual enquiry, for Congress in the first instance with subsequent judicial review looking only to the rationality of the congressional conclusion, but one of a rather different sort, dependent upon a uniquely judicial competence.

This new characterization of substantial effects has no support in our cases (the self-fulfilling prophecies of *Lopez* aside), least of all those the majority cites. Perhaps this explains why the majority is not content to rest on its cited precedent but claims a textual justification for moving toward its new system of congressional deference subject to selective discounts. . . .

The premise that the enumeration of powers implies that other powers are withheld is sound; the conclusion that some particular categories of subject matter are therefore presumptively beyond the reach of the commerce power is, however, a *non sequitur*. From the fact that Art. I, Sec. 8, cl. 3 grants an authority limited to regulating commerce, it follows only that Congress may claim no authority under that section to address any subject that does not affect commerce. It does not at all follow that an activity affecting commerce nonetheless falls outside the commerce power, depending on the specific character of the activity, or the authority of a State to regulate it along with Congress. My disagreement with the majority is not, however, confined to logic, for history has shown that categorical exclusions have proven as unworkable in practice as they are unsupportable in theory.

Chief Justice MARSHALL's seminal opinion in *Gibbons v. Ogden*, [9 Wheat 1 (1824)], construed the commerce power from the start with "a breadth never yet exceeded," *Wickard v. Filburn*. In particular, it is worth noting, the Court in *Wickard* did not regard its holding as exceeding the scope of Chief Justice MARSHALL's view of interstate commerce; *Wickard* applied an aggregate effects test to ostensibly domestic, noncommercial farming consistently with Chief Justice MARSHALL's indication that the commerce power may be understood by its exclusion of subjects, among others, "which do not affect other States." This plenary view of the power has either prevailed or been acknowledged by this Court at every stage of our jurisprudence. And it was this understanding, free of categorical qualifications, that prevailed in the period after 1937 through *Lopez*, as summed up by Justice HARLAN: "Of course, the mere fact that Congress has said when particular activity shall be deemed to affect commerce does not preclude further examination by this Court. But where we find that the legislators have a rational basis for finding a chosen regulatory scheme necessary to the protection of commerce, our investigation is at an end." *Maryland v. Wirtz*, 392 U.S. 183 (1968).

Justice HARLAN spoke with the benefit of hindsight, for he had seen the result of rejecting the plenary view, and today's attempt to distinguish between primary activities affecting commerce in terms of the relatively commercial or noncommercial character of the primary conduct proscribed comes with the pedigree of near-tragedy that I outlined in *United States v. Lopez* (dissenting opinion). In the half century following the modern activation of the commerce power with passage of the Interstate Commerce Act in 1887, this Court from time to time created categorical enclaves beyond congressional reach by declaring such activities as "mining," "production," "manufacturing," and union membership to be outside the definition of "commerce" and by limiting application of the effects test to "direct" rather than "indirect" commercial consequences. See, e.g., *United States v. E. C. Knight Co.*, 156 U.S. 1 (1895) (narrowly construing the Sherman Antitrust Act in light of the distinction between "commerce" and "manufacture"); *Hammer v. Dagenhart*, 247 U.S. 251 (1918) (invalidating law prohibiting interstate shipment of goods manufactured with child labor as a regulation of "manufacture"); *A. L. A. Schechter Poultry Corp. v. United States*, 295 U.S. 495 (1935) (invalidating regulation of activities that only "indirectly" affected commerce); *Carter v. Carter Coal Co.*, 298 U.S. 238 (1936) (holding that regulation of unfair labor practices in mining regulated "production," not "commerce").

Since adherence to these formalistically contrived confines of commerce power in large measure provoked the judicial crisis of 1937, one might reasonably have doubted that Members of this Court would ever again toy with a return to the days before *NLRB v. Jones & Laughlin Steel Corp.*, 301 U.S. 1 (1937), which brought the earlier and nearly disastrous experiment to an end. And yet today's decision can only be seen as a step toward recapturing the prior mistakes. . . .

Why is the majority tempted to reject the lesson so painfully learned in 1937? An answer emerges from contrasting *Wickard* with one of the predecessor cases it superseded. It was obvious in *Wickard* that growing wheat for consumption right on the farm was not "commerce" in the common vocabulary, but that did not matter constitutionally so long as the aggregated activity of domestic wheat growing affected commerce substantially. Just a few years before *Wickard*, however, it had certainly been no less obvious that "mining" practices could substantially affect commerce, even though *Carter Coal Co.* had held mining regulation beyond the national commerce power. When we try to fathom the difference between the two cases, it is clear that they did not go in different directions because the *Carter Coal* Court could not understand a causal connection that the *Wickard* Court could grasp; the difference, rather, turned on the fact that the Court in *Carter Coal* had a reason for trying to maintain its categorical, formalistic distinction, while that reason had been abandoned by the time *Wickard* was decided. The reason was laissez-faire economics, the point of which was to keep government interference to a minimum. The Court in *Carter Coal* was still trying to create a laissez-faire world out of the 20th-century economy, and formalistic commercial distinctions were thought to be useful instruments in achieving that object. The Court in *Wickard* knew it could not do any such thing and in the aftermath of the New Deal had long since stopped attempting the impossible. Without the animating economic theory, there was no point in contriving formalisms in a war with Chief Justice MARSHALL's conception of the commerce power.

If we now ask why the formalistic economic/noneconomic distinction might matter today, after its rejection in *Wickard*, the answer is not that the majority fails to see causal connections in an integrated economic world. The answer is that in the minds of the majority there is a new animating theory that makes categorical formalism seem useful again. Just as the old formalism had value in the service of an economic conception, the new one is useful in serving a conception of federalism. It is the instrument by which assertions of national power are to be limited in favor of preserving a supposedly discernible, proper sphere of state autonomy to legislate or refrain from legislating as the individual States see fit. The legitimacy of the Court's current emphasis on the noncommercial nature of regulated activity, then, does not turn on any logic serving the text of the Commerce Clause or on the realism of the majority's view of the national economy. The essential issue is rather the strength of the majority's claim to have a constitutional warrant for its current conception of a federal relationship enforceable by this Court through limits on otherwise plenary commerce power. This conception is the subject of the majority's second categorical discount applied today to the facts bearing on the substantial effects test.

The Court finds it relevant that the statute addresses conduct traditionally subject to state prohibition under domestic criminal law, a fact said to have some heightened significance when the violent conduct in question is not itself aimed directly at interstate commerce or its instrumentalities. Again, history seems to be recycling, for the theory of traditional state concern as grounding a limiting principle has been rejected previously, and more than once. . . .

The objection to reviving traditional state spheres of action as a consideration in commerce analysis, however, not only rests on the portent of incoherence, but is compounded by a further defect just as fundamental. The defect, in essence, is the majority's rejection of the Founders' considered judgment that politics, not judicial review, should mediate between state and national interests as the strength and legislative jurisdiction of the National Government inevitably increased through the expected growth of the national economy. Whereas today's majority takes a leaf from the book of the old judicial economists in saying that the Court should somehow draw the line to keep the federal relationship in a proper balance, Madison, Wilson, and MARSHALL understood the Constitution very differently.

Although Madison had emphasized the conception of a National Government of discrete powers (a conception that a number of the ratifying conventions thought was too indeterminate to protect civil liberties), Madison himself must have sensed the potential scope of some of the powers granted (such as the authority to regulate commerce), for he took care in The Federalist No. 46 to hedge his argument for limited power by explaining the importance of national politics in protecting the States' interests. The National Government "will partake sufficiently of the spirit [of the States], to be disinclined to invade the rights of the individual States, or the prerogatives of their governments." . . .

Politics as the moderator of the congressional employment of the commerce power was the theme many years later in *Wickard*, for after the Court acknowledged the breadth of the *Gibbons* formulation it invoked Chief Justice MARSHALL yet again in adding that "(h)e made emphatic the embracing and penetrating nature of this power by warning that effective restraints on its exercise must proceed from political rather than judicial processes." *Wickard*.

As with "conflicts of economic interest," so with supposed conflicts of sovereign political interests implicated by the Commerce Clause: the Constitution remits them to politics. The point can be put no more clearly than the Court put it the last time it repudiated the notion that some state activities categorically defied the commerce power as understood in accordance with generally accepted concepts. [In *Garcia v. San Antonio Metropolitan Transit Authority*, 469 U.S.

528 (1985), the Court] concluded that "the Framers chose to rely on a federal system in which special restraints on federal power over the States inhered principally in the workings of the National Government itself, rather than in discrete limitations on the objects of federal authority. State sovereign interests, then, are more properly protected by procedural safeguards inherent in the structure of the federal system than by judicially created limitations on federal power." . . .

All of this convinces me that today's ebb of the commerce power rests on error, and at the same time leads me to doubt that the majority's view will prove to be enduring law. There is yet one more reason for doubt. Although we sense the presence of *Carter Coal*, *Schechter*, and [*National League of Cities v.*] *Usery* [426 U.S. 833 (1976)], once again, the majority embraces them only at arm's-length. Where such decisions once stood for rules, today's opinion points to considerations by which substantial effects are discounted. Cases standing for the sufficiency of substantial effects are not overruled; cases overruled since 1937 are not quite revived. The Court's thinking betokens less clearly a return to the conceptual straitjackets of *Schechter* and *Carter Coal* and *Usery* than to something like the unsteady state of obscenity law between *Redrup v. New York*, 386 U.S. 767 (1967), and *Miller v. California*, 413 U.S. 15 (1973), a period in which the failure to provide a workable definition left this Court to review each case ad hoc. As our predecessors learned then, the practice of such ad hoc review cannot preserve the distinction between the judicial and the legislative, and this Court, in any event, lacks the institutional capacity to maintain such a regime for very long. This one will end when the majority realizes that the conception of the commerce power for which it entertains hopes would inevitably fail the test expressed in Justice HOLMES's statement that "[t]he first call of a theory of law is that it should fit the facts." The facts that cannot be ignored today are the facts of integrated national commerce and a political relationship between States and Nation much affected by their respective treasuries and constitutional modifications adopted by the people. The federalism of some earlier time is no more adequate to account for those facts today than the theory of laissez-faire was able to govern the national economy 70 years ago.

Justice BREYER, with whom Justice STEVENS joins, and with whom Justice SOUTER and Justice GINSBURG join as to Part I-A, dissenting.

The majority holds that the federal commerce power does not extend to such "noneconomic" activities as "noneconomic, violent criminal conduct" that significantly affects interstate commerce only if we "aggregate" the interstate "effect[s]" of individual instances. Justice SOUTER explains why history, precedent, and legal logic militate against the majority's approach. I agree and join his opinion. I add that the majority's holding illustrates the difficulty of finding a workable judicial Commerce Clause touchstone—a set of comprehensible interpretive rules that courts might use to impose some meaningful limit, but not too great a limit, upon the scope of the legislative authority that the Commerce Clause delegates to Congress.

Consider the problems. The "economic/noneconomic" distinction is not easy to apply. Does the local street corner mugger engage in "economic" activity or "noneconomic" activity when he mugs for money? See *Perez v. United States*,

402 U.S. 146 (1971) (aggregating local "loan sharking" instances); *United States v. Lopez*, 514 U.S. 549 (1995) (loan sharking is economic because it consists of "intrastate extortionate credit transactions"). Would evidence that desire for economic domination underlies many brutal crimes against women save the present statute?

The line becomes yet harder to draw given the need for exceptions. The Court itself would permit Congress to aggregate, hence regulate, "noneconomic" activity taking place at economic establishments. See *Heart of Atlanta Motel, Inc. v. United States*, 379 U.S. 241 (1964) (upholding civil rights laws forbidding discrimination at local motels); *Katzenbach v. McClung*, 379 U.S. 294 (1964) (same for restaurants); *Lopez* (recognizing congressional power to aggregate, hence forbid, noneconomically motivated discrimination at public accommodations).

More important, why should we give critical constitutional importance to the economic, or noneconomic, nature of an interstate-commerce-affecting cause? If chemical emanations through indirect environmental change cause identical, severe commercial harm outside a State, why should it matter whether local factories or home fireplaces release them? The Constitution itself refers only to Congress' power to "regulate Commerce . . . among the several States," and to make laws "necessary and proper" to implement that power. The language says nothing about either the local nature, or the economic nature, of an interstate-commerce-affecting cause. . . .

Most important, the Court's complex rules seem unlikely to help secure the very object that they seek, namely, the protection of "areas of traditional state regulation" from federal intrusion. The Court's rules, even if broadly interpreted, are underinclusive. The local pickpocket is no less a traditional subject of state regulation than is the local gender-motivated assault. Regardless, the Court reaffirms, as it should, Congress' well-established and frequently exercised power to enact laws that satisfy a commerce-related jurisdictional prerequisite—for example, that some item relevant to the federally regulated activity has at some time crossed a state line.

And in a world where most everyday products or their component parts cross interstate boundaries, Congress will frequently find it possible to redraft a statute using language that ties the regulation to the interstate movement of some relevant object, thereby regulating local criminal activity or, for that matter, family affairs. Although this possibility does not give the Federal Government the power to regulate everything, it means that any substantive limitation will apply randomly in terms of the interests the majority seeks to protect. How much would be gained, for example, were Congress to reenact the present law in the form of "An Act Forbidding Violence Against Women Perpetrated at Public Accommodations or by Those Who Have Moved in, or through the Use of Items that Have Moved in, Interstate Commerce"? Complex Commerce Clause rules creating fine distinctions that achieve only random results do little to further the important federalist interests that called them into being. That is why modern (pre-*Lopez*) case law rejected them. . . .

For these reasons, as well as those set forth by Justice SOUTER, this statute falls well within Congress's Commerce Clause authority, and I dissent from the Court's contrary conclusion. . . .

# 7

## THE STATES AND AMERICAN FEDERALISM

### A. STATES' POWER OVER COMMERCE AND REGULATION

#### THE DEVELOPMENT OF LAW

Other Rulings on State Regulatory Powers
in Alleged Conflict with Federal Legislation

| Case | Vote | Ruling |
|------|------|--------|
| *United States v. Locke*, 120 S.Ct. 1135 (2000) | | The Court unanimously struck down Washington's navigational regulations as preempted by the Oil Pollution Act of 1990. Following the oil spill of the Exxon *Valdez* in 1989, both Congress and Washington enacted laws to protect the environment from future oil spills, but the state's regulations were more extensive and stringent than those set forth in federal statutes and international treaties. |
| *Crosby v. National Foreign Trade Council*, 120 S.Ct. 2288 (2000) | | The Court invalidated Massachusetts's 1996 law restricting public agencies from contracting with companies that also conduct business with Burma—a repressive Southeast Asian country that changed its name to Myanmar in 1989. Writing for the Court, Justice Souter held that a 1996 federal statute imposing a set of mandatory and conditional sanctions on Burma preempted the state law. The fact that Congress had not expressly preempted state laws on the matter was deemed irrelevant because Massachusetts's law ran contrary to Congress's authorization for the President to set and adjust the nation's policy toward Burma. |

## B. THE TENTH AMENDMENT AND THE STATES

Continuing a recent trend, Chief Justice Rehnquist again commanded bare majorities for limiting congressional power and buttressing state authority. In *Florida Prepaid Postsecondary Education Expense Board v. College Savings Bank*, 119 S.Ct. 2199 (1999), Chief Justice Rehnquist, joined by Justices Kennedy, O'Connor, Scalia, and Thomas, held that Congress exceeded its powers in abrogating states' sovereign immunity when enacting the Patent and Plant Variety Protection Remedy Clarification Act. Relying on the five to four decision in *Seminole Tribe of Florida v. Florida*, 116 S.Ct. 1114 (1996) (excerpted in Vol. 1, Ch. 6), the chief justice ruled that Congress had exceeded its power under Article I and, drawing on the Court's analysis and holding in *City of Borne v. Flores*, 521 U.S. 507 (1997) (excerpted in Vol. 2, Ch. 6), also ruled that Congress had exceeded its enforcement power under Section 5 of the Fourteenth Amendment. Here, as in other recent rulings supporting states' rights and limiting congressional power, Justices Stevens, Souter, Ginsburg, and Breyer dissented.

In another major decision upholding state authority, *Alden v. Maine* (1999) (excerpted below), Justice Kennedy ruled that the Constitution's "structure and history" shields states not only from being sued in federal courts, but also makes them immune from lawsuits filed in state courts that seek to enforce federal rights against them. Here, Maine's probation officers had sought to enforce a federal right to be paid for overtime work. Once again, Justices Stevens, Souter, Ginsburg, and Breyer dissented. And in a related ruling bearing on lawsuits filed against states, the Court held, in *Vermont Agency of Natural Resources v. United States ex rel. Stevens*, 120 S.Ct. 1858 (2000), that a private individual may not bring a suit in federal court on behalf of the U.S. government against a state or state agency under the False Claims Act. Stevens had sued the Vermont Agency of Natural Resources, alleging that it had submitted false claims to the Environmental Protection Agency in connection with federal grants it administers. Writing for the Court, Justice Scalia held that a sovereign state is not a legal "person" subject to suit under the act. Justices Souter and Stevens dissented.

In its 1999–2000 term Chief Justice Rehnquist's bare majority further extended the doctrine in *Seminole Tribe*, *City of Boerne*, and *Alden* in *Kimel v. Florida Board of Regents* (excerpted below). Writing for the Court, Justice O'Connor held that Congress exceeded its powers in abrogating states' sovereign immunity under the Eleventh Amendment in extending the Age Discrimination in Employment Act to state employees and ruled that state employees could not bring suits in federal courts to enforce provisions of the law. Yet again, Justices Stevens, Breyer, Ginsburg, and Souter dissented.

In its 2000–2001 term, the Court will consider whether the Americans with Disabilities Act (ADA) and the Rehabilitation Act (RA) abrogated states' sovereign immunity under the Eleventh Amendment, in *University of Alabama at Birmingham Board of Trustees v. Garrett*. A federal district court held that states are immune from suits claiming violations of ADA and RA, but the Court of Appeals for the Eleventh Circuit reversed, holding that, consistent with *Seminole Tribe*, Congress properly and explicitly abrogated states' immunity and properly exercised its enforcement power under Section 5 of the Fourteenth Amendment.

## *Alden v. Maine*
### 119 S.Ct. 2240 (1999)

The pertinent facts are discussed by Justice Kennedy in his opinion for the Court, affirming the decision of Maine Supreme Judicial Court. The Court's decision was five to four. Justice Souter filed a dissenting opinion, which was joined by Justices Stevens, Ginsburg, and Breyer.

Justice KENNEDY delivered the opinion of the Court.

In 1992, petitioners, a group of probation officers, filed suit against their employer, the State of Maine, in the United States District Court for the District of Maine. The officers alleged the State had violated the overtime provisions of the Fair Labor Standards Act of 1938 (FLSA), and sought compensation and liquidated damages. While the suit was pending, this Court decided *Seminole Tribe of Fla. v. Florida*, 517 U.S. 44 (1996), which made it clear that Congress lacks power under Article I to abrogate the States' sovereign immunity from suits commenced or prosecuted in the federal courts. Upon consideration of *Seminole Tribe*, the District Court dismissed petitioners' action, and the Court of Appeals affirmed. Petitioners then filed the same action in state court. The state trial court dismissed the suit on the basis of sovereign immunity, and the Maine Supreme Judicial Court affirmed. . . .

We hold that the powers delegated to Congress under Article I of the United States Constitution do not include the power to subject nonconsenting States to private suits for damages in state courts. We decide as well that the State of Maine has not consented to suits for overtime pay and liquidated damages under the FLSA. On these premises we affirm the judgment sustaining dismissal of the suit.

The Eleventh Amendment makes explicit reference to the States' immunity from suits "commenced or prosecuted against one of the United States by Citizens of another State, or by Citizens or Subjects of any Foreign State." We have, as a result, sometimes referred to the States' immunity from suit as "Eleventh Amendment immunity." The phrase is convenient shorthand but something of a misnomer, for the sovereign immunity of the States neither derives from nor is limited by the terms of the Eleventh Amendment. Rather, as the Constitution's structure, and its history, and the authoritative interpretations by this Court make clear, the States' immunity from suit is a fundamental aspect of the sovereignty which the States enjoyed before the ratification of the Constitution, and which they retain today (either literally or by virtue of their admission into the Union upon an equal footing with the other States) except as altered by the plan of the Convention or certain constitutional Amendments.

Although the Constitution establishes a National Government with broad, often plenary authority over matters within its recognized competence, the founding document "specifically recognizes the States as sovereign entities." *Seminole Tribe of Fla.* Various textual provisions of the Constitution assume the States' continued existence and active participation in the fundamental processes of governance. See *Printz v. United States*, 521 U.S. 898 (1997) (citing Art. III, Sec. 2; Art. IV, Secs. 2–4; Art. V). The limited and enumerated powers granted to the Legislative, Executive, and Judicial Branches of the National Government, moreover, underscore the vital role reserved to the States by the constitutional design. Any doubt regarding the constitutional role of the States as sovereign entities is removed by the Tenth Amendment, which, like the other provisions of the Bill of Rights, was enacted to allay lingering concerns about the extent of the national power. The Amendment confirms the promise implicit in the original document: "The powers not delegated to the United States by the Constitution, nor prohibited by it to the States, are reserved to the States respectively, or to the people."

The federal system established by our Constitution preserves the sovereign status of the States in two ways. First, it reserves to them a substantial portion of the Nation's primary sovereignty, together with the dignity and essential attributes inhering in that status. . . .

Second, even as to matters within the competence of the National Government, the constitutional design secures the founding generation's rejection of "the concept of a central government that would act upon and through the States" in favor of "a system in which the State and Federal Governments would exercise concurrent authority over the people—who were, in Hamilton's words, "the only proper objects of government." *Printz.* In this the founders achieved a deliberate departure from the Articles of Confederation: Experience under the Articles had "exploded on all hands" the "practicality of making laws, with coercive sanctions, for the States as political bodies." . . .

The generation that designed and adopted our federal system considered immunity from private suits central to sovereign dignity. When the Constitution was ratified, it was well established in English law that the Crown could not be sued without consent in its own courts. See *Chisholm v. Georgia*, 2 Dall. 419 (1793) (IREDELL, J., dissenting). . . .

[The Court's decision in *Chisholm v. Georgia* met with wide spread opposition and resulted in the adoption and ratification of the Eleventh Amendment, guaranteeing states' sovereign immunity against lawsuits by citizens of other states.] Each House spent but a single day discussing the Amendment, and the vote in each House was close to unanimous. All attempts to weaken the Amendment were defeated. . . .

It might be argued that the *Chisholm* decision was a correct interpretation of the constitutional design and that the Eleventh Amendment represented a deviation from the original understanding. This, however, seems unsupportable. First, despite the opinion of Justice IREDELL, the majority failed to address either the practice or the understanding that prevailed in the States at the time the Constitution was adopted. Second, even a casual reading of the opinions suggests the majority suspected the decision would be unpopular and surprising. . . .

The text and history of the Eleventh Amendment also suggest that Congress acted not to change but to restore the original constitutional design. Although earlier drafts of the Amendment had been phrased as express limits on the judicial power granted in Article III, the adopted text addressed the proper interpretation of that provision of the original Constitution, see U.S. Const., Amdt. 11 ("The Judicial Power of the United States shall not be construed to extend to any suit in law or equity, commenced or prosecuted against one of the United States"). By its terms, then, the Eleventh Amendment did not redefine the federal judicial power but instead overruled the Court. . . .

The Court has been consistent in interpreting the adoption of the Eleventh Amendment as conclusive evidence "that the decision in *Chisholm* was contrary to the well-understood meaning of the Constitution," *Seminole Tribe*, and that the views expressed by Hamilton, Madison, and Marshall during the ratification debates, and by Justice IREDELL in his dissenting opinion in *Chisholm*, reflect the original understanding of the Constitution. In accordance with this understanding, we have recognized a "presumption that no anomalous and unheard-of proceedings or suits were intended to be raised up by the Constitution—anomalous and unheard of when the constitution was adopted." As a consequence, we have looked to "history and experience, and the established order of things," rather than "[a]dhering to the mere letter" of the Eleventh Amendment in determining the scope of the States' constitutional immunity from suit. . . .

[Prior] holdings reflect a settled doctrinal understanding, consistent with the views of the leading advocates of the Constitution's ratification, that sovereign immunity derives not from the Eleventh Amendment but from the structure of the original Constitution itself. The Eleventh Amendment confirmed rather than established sovereign immunity as a constitutional principle; it follows that the scope of the States' immunity from suit is demarcated not by the text of the Amendment alone but by fundamental postulates implicit in the constitutional design. . . .

In this case we must determine whether Congress has the power, under Article I, to subject nonconsenting States to private suits in their own courts. As the foregoing discussion makes clear, the fact that the Eleventh Amendment by its terms limits only "[t]he Judicial power of the United States" does not resolve the question. To rest on the words of the Amendment alone would be to engage in the type of ahistorical literalism we have rejected in interpreting the scope of the States' sovereign immunity since the discredited decision in *Chisholm*.

While the constitutional principle of sovereign immunity does pose a bar to federal jurisdiction over suits against nonconsenting States, this is not the only structural basis of sovereign immunity implicit in the constitutional design. Rather, "[t]here is also the postulate that States of the Union, still possessing attributes of sovereignty, shall be immune from suits, without their consent, save where there has been a surrender of this immunity in the plan of the convention." This separate and distinct structural principle is not directly related to the scope of the judicial power established by Article III, but inheres in the system of federalism established by the Constitution. In exercising its Article I powers Congress may subject the States to private suits in their own courts only if there is "compelling evidence" that the States were required to surrender this power to Congress pursuant to the constitutional design.

Petitioners contend the text of the Constitution and our recent sovereign immunity decisions establish that the States were required to relinquish this portion of their sovereignty. [But, we disagree.] The Constitution, by delegating to Congress the power to establish the supreme law of the land when acting within its enumerated powers, does not foreclose a State from asserting immunity to claims arising under federal law merely because that law derives not from the State itself but from the national power. A contrary view could not be reconciled with . . . *Employees of Dept. of Public Health and Welfare of Mo. v. Department of Public Health and Welfare of Mo.*, 411 U.S. 279 (1973), which recognized that the FLSA was binding upon Missouri but nevertheless upheld the State's immunity to a private suit to recover under that Act; or with numerous other decisions to the same effect. We reject any contention that substantive federal law by its own force necessarily overrides the sovereign immunity of the States. When a State asserts its immunity to suit, the question is not the primacy of federal law but the implementation of the law in a manner consistent with the constitutional sovereignty of the States. . . .

Whether Congress has authority under Article I to abrogate a State's immunity from suit in its own courts is, then, a question of first impression. In determining whether there is "compelling evidence" that this derogation of the States' sovereignty is "inherent in the constitutional compact," we continue our discussion of history, practice, precedent, and the structure of the Constitution.

We look first to evidence of the original understanding of the Constitution. Petitioners contend that because the ratification debates and the events surrounding the adoption of the Eleventh Amendment focused on the States' immunity from suit in federal courts, the historical record gives no instruction as to the founding generation's intent to preserve the States' immunity from suit in their own courts.

We believe, however, that the founders' silence is best explained by the simple fact that no one, not even the Constitution's most ardent opponents, suggested the document might strip the States of the immunity. In light of the overriding concern regarding the States' war-time debts, together with the well known creativity, foresight, and vivid imagination of the Constitution's opponents, the silence is most instructive. It suggests the sovereign's right to assert immunity from suit in its own courts was a principle so well established that no one conceived it would be altered by the new Constitution. . . .

[W]hile the Eleventh Amendment by its terms addresses only "the Judicial power of the United States," nothing in *Chisholm*, the catalyst for the Amendment, suggested the States were not immune from suits in their own courts. . . .

In light of the language of the Constitution and the historical context, it is quite apparent why neither the ratification debates nor the language of the Eleventh Amendment addressed the States' immunity from suit in their own courts. The concerns voiced at the ratifying conventions, the furor raised by *Chisholm*, and the speed and unanimity with which the Amendment was adopted, moreover, underscore the jealous care with which the founding generation sought to preserve the sovereign immunity of the States. . . .

Our final consideration is whether a congressional power to subject nonconsenting States to private suits in their own courts is consistent with the structure of the Constitution. We look both to the essential principles of federalism and to the special role of the state courts in the constitutional design. . . .

Petitioners contend that immunity from suit in federal court suffices to preserve the dignity of the States. Private suits against nonconsenting States, however, present "the indignity of subjecting a State to the coercive process of judicial tribunals at the instance of private parties," *In re Ayers*, [123 U.S. 443 (1887)], regardless of the forum. Not only must a State defend or default but also it must face the prospect of being thrust, by federal fiat and against its will, into the disfavored status of a debtor, subject to the power of private citizens to levy on its treasury or perhaps even government buildings or property which the State administers on the public's behalf. . . .

A general federal power to authorize private suits for money damages would place unwarranted strain on the States' ability to govern in accordance with the will of their citizens. Today, as at the time of the founding, the allocation of scarce resources among competing needs and interests lies at the heart of the political process. While the judgment creditor of the State may have a legitimate claim for compensation, other important needs and worthwhile ends compete for access to the public fisc. Since all cannot be satisfied in full, it is inevitable that difficult decisions involving the most sensitive and political of judgments must be made. If the principle of representative government is to be preserved to the States, the balance between competing interests must be reached after deliberation by the political process established by the citizens of the State, not by judicial decree mandated by the Federal Government and invoked by the private citizen.

By "split[ting] the atom of sovereignty," the founders established "two orders of government, each with its own direct relationship, its own privity, its own set of mutual rights and obligations to the people who sustain it and are governed by it." *Saenz v. Roe*, 526 U.S. [119 S.Ct. 1518] (1999). When the Federal Government asserts authority over a State's most fundamental political processes, it strikes at the heart of the political accountability so essential to our liberty and republican form of government.

The asserted authority would blur not only the distinct responsibilities of the State and National Governments but also the separate duties of the judicial and political branches of the state governments, displacing "state decisions that 'go to the heart of representative government.'" *Gregory v. Ashcroft*, 501 U.S. 452 (1991). A State is entitled to order the processes of its own governance, assigning to the political branches, rather than the courts, the responsibility for directing the payment of debts. If Congress could displace a State's allocation of governmental power and responsibility, the judicial branch of the State, whose legitimacy derives from fidelity to the law, would be compelled to assume a role not only foreign to its experience but beyond its competence as defined by the very constitution from which its existence derives. . . .

In light of history, practice, precedent, and the structure of the Constitution, we hold that the States retain immunity from private suit in their own courts, an immunity beyond the congressional power to abrogate by Article I legislation.

The constitutional privilege of a State to assert its sovereign immunity in its own courts does not confer upon the State a concomitant right to disregard the Constitution or valid federal law. The States and their officers are bound by obligations imposed by the Constitution and by federal statutes that comport with the constitutional design. We are unwilling to assume the States will refuse to honor the Constitution or obey the binding laws of the United States.

Sovereign immunity, moreover, does not bar all judicial review of state compliance with the Constitution and valid federal law. Rather, certain limits are implicit in the constitutional principle of state sovereign immunity.

The first of these limits is that sovereign immunity bars suits only in the absence of consent. Many States, on their own initiative, have enacted statutes consenting to a wide variety of suits. The rigors of sovereign immunity are thus "mitigated by a sense of justice which has continually expanded by consent the suability of the sovereign." *Great Northern Life Ins. Co.*[*v. Read*, 322 U.S. 47 (1944)]. Nor, subject to constitutional limitations, does the Federal Government lack the authority or means to seek the States' voluntary consent to private suits. Cf. *South Dakota v. Dole*, 483 U.S. 203 (1987).

We have held also that in adopting the Fourteenth Amendment, the people required the States to surrender a portion of the sovereignty that had been preserved to them by the original Constitution, so that Congress may authorize private suits against nonconsenting States pursuant to its Section 5 enforcement power. By imposing explicit limits on the powers of the States and granting Congress the power to enforce them, the Amendment "fundamentally altered the balance of state and federal power struck by the Constitution." *Seminole Tribe.* When Congress enacts appropriate legislation to enforce this Amendment, see *City of Boerne v. Flores*, 521 U.S. 507 (1997), federal interests are paramount, and Congress may assert an authority over the States which would be otherwise unauthorized by the Constitution.

The second important limit to the principle of sovereign immunity is that it bars suits against States but not lesser entities. The immunity does not extend to suits prosecuted against a municipal corporation or other governmental entity which is not an arm of the State. Nor does sovereign immunity bar all suits against state officers. Some suits against state officers are barred by the rule that sovereign immunity is not limited to suits which name the State as a party if the suits are, in fact, against the State. The rule, however, does not bar certain actions against state officers for injunctive or declaratory relief. Compare *Ex parte Young*, 209 U.S. 123 (1908), and *In re Ayers*, supra, with *Seminole Tribe*, supra, and *Edelman v. Jordan*, 415 U.S. 651 (1974). Even a suit for money damages may be prosecuted against a state officer in his individual capacity for unconstitutional or wrongful conduct fairly attributable to the officer himself, so long as the relief is sought not from the state treasury but from the officer personally. . . .

The sole remaining question is whether Maine has waived its immunity. . . . The State, we conclude, has not consented to suit. . . .

[Finally, t]he State of Maine has not questioned Congress' power to prescribe substantive rules of federal law to which it must comply. Despite an initial good-faith disagreement about the requirements of the FLSA, it is conceded by all that the State has altered its conduct so that its compliance with federal law cannot now be questioned. The Solicitor General of the United States has appeared before this Court, however, and asserted that the federal interest in compensating the States' employees for alleged past violations of federal law is so compelling that the sovereign State of Maine must be stripped of its immunity and subjected to suit in its own courts by its own employees. Yet, despite specific statutory authorization, the United States apparently found the same interests insufficient to justify sending even a single attorney to Maine to prosecute this litigation. The difference between a suit by the United States on behalf of the employees and a suit by the employees implicates a rule that the National Government must itself deem the case of sufficient importance to take action against the State; and history, precedent, and the structure of the Constitution make clear that, under the plan of the Convention, the States have consented to suits of the first kind but not of the second. The judgment of the Supreme Judicial Court of Maine is affirmed.

Justice SOUTER, with whom Justice STEVENS, Justice GINSBURG, and Justice BREYER join, dissenting.

In *Seminole Tribe of Fla. v. Florida*, 517 U.S. 44 (1996), a majority of this Court invoked the Eleventh Amendment to declare that the federal judicial power under Article III of the Constitution does not reach a private action against a State, even on a federal question. In the Court's conception, however, the Eleventh Amendment was understood as having been enhanced by a "background principle" of state sovereign immunity (understood as immunity to suit) that operated beyond its limited codification in the Amendment, dealing solely with federal citizen-state diversity jurisdiction. To the *Seminole Tribe* dissenters, of whom I was one, the Court's enhancement of the Amendment was at odds with constitutional history and at war with the conception of divided sovereignty that is the essence of American federalism.

Today's issue arises naturally in the aftermath of the decision in *Seminole Tribe*. . . . In thus complementing its earlier decision, the Court of course confronts the fact that the state forum renders the Eleventh Amendment beside the point, and it has responded by discerning a simpler and more straightforward theory of state sovereign immunity than it found in *Seminole Tribe*: a State's sovereign immunity from all individual suits is a "fundamental aspect" of state sovereignty "confirm[ed]" by the Tenth Amendment. As a consequence, *Seminole Tribe*'s contorted reliance on the Eleventh Amendment and its background was presumably unnecessary; the Tenth would have done the work with an economy that the majority in *Seminole Tribe* would have welcomed. Indeed, if the Court's current reasoning is correct, the Eleventh Amendment itself was unnecessary. Whatever Article III may originally have said about the federal judicial power, the embarrassment to the State of Georgia occasioned by attempts in federal court to enforce the State's war debt could easily have been avoided if only the Court that decided *Chisholm v. Georgia*, 2 Dall. 419 (1793), had understood a State's inherent, Tenth Amendment right to be free of any judicial power, whether the court be state or federal, and whether the cause of action arise under state or federal law.

The sequence of the Court's positions prompts a suspicion of error, and skepticism is confirmed by scrutiny of the Court's efforts to justify its holding. There is no evidence that the Tenth Amendment constitutionalized a concept of sovereign immunity as inherent in the notion of statehood, and no evidence that any concept of inherent sovereign immunity was understood historically to apply when the sovereign sued was not the font of the law. Nor does the Court fare any better with its subsidiary lines of reasoning, that the state-court action is barred by the scheme of American federalism, a result supposedly confirmed by a history largely devoid of precursors to the action considered here. The Court's federalism ignores the accepted authority of Congress to bind States under the FLSA and to provide for enforcement of federal rights in state court. The Court's history simply disparages the capacity of the Constitution to order relationships in a Republic that has changed since the founding.

On each point the Court has raised it is mistaken, and I respectfully dissent from its judgment.

# Kimel v. Florida Board of Regents
## 120 S.Ct. 631 (2000)

J. Daniel Kimel, Jr., and several other professors and librarians, all over the age of 40, sued the Florida Board of Regents for age discrimination under the Age Discrimination in Employment Act of 1967 (ADEA). That law, as subsequently amended in 1974 to apply to state and local governments, makes it unlawful for an employer "to fail or refuse to hire or discharge any individual or otherwise discriminate against any individual 'because of such individual's age.'" In a separate suit, state employees sued Alabama for age discrimination. The federal district courts' decisions in these cases were consolidated on appeal before the Court of Appeals for the Eleventh Circuit, which held that the ADEA did not abrogate states' sovereign immunity under the Eleventh Amendment and dismissed the suits. That decision was appealed, and the Supreme Court granted review.

The appellate court's decision was affirmed in an opinion delivered by Justice O'Connor. Justice Stevens filed an opinion in part concurring and dissenting, which Justices Breyer, Ginsburg, and Souter joined. Justice Thomas, joined by Justice Kennedy, issued an opinion in part concurring and dissenting.

Justice O'CONNOR delivered the opinion of the Court.

Although today's cases concern suits brought by citizens against their own States, this Court has long "'understood the Eleventh Amendment to stand not so much for what it says, but for the presupposition—which it confirms.'" *Seminole Tribe of Florida v. Florida*, 517 U.S. 44 (1996). Accordingly, for over a century now, we have made clear that the Constitution does not provide for federal jurisdiction over suits against nonconsenting States. Petitioners nevertheless contend that the States of Alabama and Florida must defend the present suits on the merits because Congress abrogated their Eleventh Amendment immunity in the ADEA. To determine whether petitioners are correct, we must resolve two predicate questions: first, whether Congress unequivocally expressed its intent to abrogate that immunity; and second, if it did, whether Congress acted pursuant to a valid grant of constitutional authority.

To determine whether a federal statute properly subjects States to suits by individuals, we apply a "simple but stringent test: 'Congress may abrogate the States' constitutionally secured immunity from suit in federal court only by making its intention unmistakably clear in the language of the statute.'" *Dellmuth v. Muth*, 491 U.S. 223 (1989). We agree with petitioners that the ADEA satisfies that test. . . .

This is not the first time we have considered the constitutional validity of the 1974 extension of the ADEA to state and local governments. In *EEOC v. Wyoming*, 460 U.S. 226 (1983), we held that the ADEA constitutes a valid exercise of Congress' power "[t]o regulate Commerce among the several States," and that the Act did not transgress any external restraints imposed on the commerce power by the Tenth Amendment. Because we found the ADEA valid under Congress' Commerce Clause power, we concluded that it was unnecessary to determine whether the Act also could be supported by Congress' power under Section 5 of the Fourteenth Amendment. Resolution of today's cases requires us to decide that question.

In *Seminole Tribe*, we held that Congress lacks power under Article I to abrogate the States' sovereign immunity. . . . Under our firmly established precedent then, if the ADEA rests solely on Congress' Article I commerce power, the private petitioners in today's cases cannot maintain their suits against their state employers.

Justice STEVENS disputes that well-established precedent again. . . . In *Alden* [*v. Maine*, 119 S.Ct. 2240 (1999)], we explained that, "[a]lthough the sovereign immunity of the States derives at least in part from the common-law tradition, the structure and history of the Constitution make clear that the immunity exists today by constitutional design." For purposes of today's decision, it is sufficient to note that we have on more than one occasion explained the substantial reasons for adhering to that constitutional design. . . . Today we adhere to our holding in *Seminole Tribe*: Congress' powers under Article I of the Constitution do not include the power to subject States to suit at the hands of private individuals.

Section 5 of the Fourteenth Amendment, however, does grant Congress the authority to abrogate the States' sovereign immunity. In *Fitzpatrick v. Bitzer*, 427 U.S. 445 (1976), we recognized that "the Eleventh Amendment, and the principle of state sovereignty which it embodies, are necessarily limited by the enforcement provisions of Section 5 of the Fourteenth Amendment." Accordingly, the private petitioners in these cases may maintain their ADEA suits against the States of Alabama and Florida if, and only if, the ADEA is appropriate legislation under Section 5. . . .

As we recognized most recently in *City of Boerne v. Flores*, 521 U.S. 507 (1997), Section 5 is an affirmative grant of power to Congress. Congress' power "to enforce" the Amendment includes the authority both to remedy and to deter violation of rights guaranteed thereunder by prohibiting a somewhat broader swath of conduct, including that which is not itself forbidden by the Amendment's text.

Nevertheless, we have also recognized that the same language that serves as the basis for the affirmative grant of congressional power also serves to limit that power. For example, Congress cannot "decree the substance of the Fourteenth Amendment's restrictions on the States. It has been given the power 'to enforce,' not the power to determine what constitutes a constitutional violation." The ultimate interpretation and determination of the Fourteenth Amendment's substantive meaning remains the province of the Judicial Branch. In *City of Boerne*, we noted that the determination whether purportedly prophylactic legislation constitutes appropriate remedial legislation, or instead effects a substantive redefinition of the Fourteenth Amendment right at issue, is often difficult. The line between the two is a fine one. Accordingly, recognizing that "Congress must have wide latitude in determining where [that line] lies," we held that "[t]here must be a congruence and proportionality between the injury to be prevented or remedied and the means adopted to that end." . . .

Applying the same "congruence and proportionality" test in these cases, we conclude that the ADEA is not "appropriate legislation" under Section 5 of the Fourteenth Amendment. Initially, the substantive requirements the ADEA imposes on state and local governments are disproportionate to any unconstitutional conduct that conceivably could be targeted by the Act. We have considered claims of unconstitutional age discrimination under the Equal Protection Clause three times. See *Gregory v. Ashcroft*, 501 U.S. 452 (1991); *Vance v. Bradley*, 440 U.S. 93 (1979); *Massachusetts Bd. of Retirement v. Murgia*, 427 U.S. 307 (1976). In all three cases, we held that the age classifications at issue did not violate the Equal Protection Clause. . . . Older persons, again, unlike those who suffer discrimination on the basis of race or gender, have not been subjected to a "'history of purposeful unequal treatment.'" Old age also does not define a discrete and insular minority because all persons, if they live out their normal life spans, will experience it. Accordingly, as we recognized in *Murgia*, *Bradley*, and *Gregory*, age is not a suspect classification under the Equal Protection Clause.

States may discriminate on the basis of age without offending the Fourteenth Amendment if the age classification in question is rationally related to a legitimate state interest. The rationality commanded by the Equal Protection Clause does not require States to match age distinctions and the legitimate interests they serve with razorlike precision. As we have explained, when conducting rational basis review "we will not overturn such [government action] unless the varying treatment of different groups or persons is so unrelated to the achievement of any combination of legitimate purposes that we can only conclude that the [government's] actions were irrational." In contrast, when a State discriminates on the basis of race or gender, we require a tighter fit between the discriminatory means and the legitimate ends they serve. Under the Fourteenth Amendment, a State may rely on age as a proxy for other qualities, abilities, or characteristics that are relevant to the State's legitimate interests. The Constitution does not preclude reliance on such generalizations. That age proves to be an inaccurate proxy in any individual case is irrelevant. Finally, because an age classification is presumptively rational, the individual challenging its constitutionality bears the burden of proving that the "facts on which the classification is apparently based could not reasonably be conceived to be true by the governmental decisionmaker." Our decisions in *Murgia*, *Bradley*, and *Gregory* illustrate these principles. In all three cases, we held that the States' reliance on broad generalizations with respect to age did not violate the Equal Protection Clause. . . . Judged against the backdrop of our equal protection jurisprudence, it is clear that the ADEA is "so out of proportion to a supposed remedial or preventive object that it cannot be understood as responsive to, or designed to prevent, unconstitutional behavior." *City of Boerne*. . . .

Finally, the United States' argument that Congress found substantial age discrimination in the private sector is beside the point. Congress made no such findings with respect to the States. . . . In light of the indiscriminate scope of the Act's substantive requirements, and the lack of evidence of widespread and unconstitutional age discrimination by the States, we hold that the ADEA is not a valid exercise of Congress' power under Section 5 of the Fourteenth Amendment. The ADEA's purported abrogation of the States' sovereign immunity is accordingly invalid. . . .

Justice STEVENS, with whom Justice SOUTER, Justice GINSBURG, and Justice BREYER join, dissenting in part and concurring in part.

Congress' power to regulate the American economy includes the power to regulate both the public and the private sectors of the labor market. Federal rules outlawing discrimination in the workplace, like the regulation of wages and hours or health and safety standards, may be enforced against public as well as private employers. Congress' power to authorize federal remedies against state agencies that violate federal statutory obligations is coextensive with its power to impose those obligations on the States in the first place. Neither the Eleventh Amendment nor the doctrine of sovereign immunity places any limit on that power. . . . .

The Eleventh Amendment simply does not support the Court's view. As has been stated before, the Amendment only places a textual limitation on the diversity jurisdiction of the federal courts. Because the Amendment is a part of the Constitution, I have never understood how its limitation on the diversity jurisdiction of federal courts defined in Article III could be "abrogated" by an Act of Congress. Here, however, private petitioners did not invoke the federal courts' diversity jurisdiction; they are citizens of the same State as the defendants and they are asserting claims that arise under federal law. Thus, today's decision (relying as it does on *Seminole Tribe*) rests entirely on a novel judicial interpretation of the doctrine of sovereign immunity, which the Court treats as though it were a constitutional precept. It is nevertheless clear to me that if Congress has the power to create the federal rights that these petitioners are asserting, it must also have the power to give the federal courts jurisdiction to remedy violations of those rights, even if it is necessary to "abrogate" the Court's "Eleventh Amendment" version of the common-law defense of sovereign immunity to do so. That is the essence of the Court's holding in *Pennsylvania v. Union Gas Co.*, 491 U.S. 1 (1989).

I remain convinced that *Union Gas* was correctly decided and that the decision of five Justices in *Seminole Tribe* to overrule that case was profoundly misguided. Despite my respect for *stare decisis*, I am unwilling to accept *Seminole Tribe* as controlling precedent. First and foremost, the reasoning of that opinion is so profoundly mistaken and so fundamentally inconsistent with the Framers' conception of the constitutional order that it has forsaken any claim to the usual deference or respect owed to decisions of this Court. . . . Further, *Seminole Tribe* is a case that will unquestionably have serious ramifications in future cases; indeed, it has already had such an effect, as in the Court's decision today and in the equally misguided opinion of *Alden v. Maine* (1999). Further still, the *Seminole Tribe* decision unnecessarily forces the Court to resolve vexing questions of constitutional law respecting Congress' Section 5 authority. Finally, by its own repeated overruling of earlier precedent, the majority has itself discounted the importance of *stare decisis* in this area of the law. The kind of judicial activism manifested in cases like *Seminole Tribe*, *Alden v. Maine*, [and] *Florida Prepaid Postsecondary Ed. Expense Bd. v. College Savings Bank*, [119 S.Ct. 2199] (1999), represents such a radical departure from the proper role of this Court that it should be opposed whenever the opportunity arises.

Accordingly, I respectfully dissent.

# 8

---

# REPRESENTATIVE GOVERNMENT, VOTING RIGHTS, AND ELECTORAL POLITICS

## A. REPRESENTATIVE GOVERNMENT AND THE FRANCHISE

THE DEVELOPMENT OF LAW

Other Rulings Interpreting the Voting Rights Act

| Case | Vote | Ruling |
| --- | --- | --- |
| *Reno v. Bossier Parish School Board*, 120 S.Ct. 866 (2000) | 5:4 | Writing for the majority, Justice Scalia ruled that Section 5 of the Voting Rights Act does |

not prohibit Department of Justice (DoJ) preclearance of a redistricting plan adopted with an ostensibly discriminatory but nonretrogressive purpose. The DoJ had objected to Bossier Parish School Board's plan to give all twelve voting districts white majorities, even though about twenty percent of the population is black. The DoJ contended that it could deny preclearance approval because the plan would dilute African American voting strength. But, Justice Scalia rejected that interpretation of the Voting Rights Act in holding that preclearance could be denied only if a redistricting plan would put blacks in a worse position or to prevent "backsliding." That narrower interpretation was deemed by the Court's majority to be justified given "the substantial federalism costs that the preclearance procedure already exacts" from state and local governments. Justices Stevens, Souter, Ginsburg, and Breyer dissented.

# B. VOTING RIGHTS AND THE REAPPORTIONMENT REVOLUTION

In its 2000–2001 term the Court will once again consider the issue of race in drawing lines for congressional districts. In *Shaw v. Reno*, 509 U.S. 630 (1993) (see Vol. 1, Ch. 8), a bare majority struck down the boundaries for North Carolina's Twelfth Congressional District because they were deemed so extraordinarily irregular in creating a majority-black district as to be unconstitutional. In *Hunt v. Cromartie* and *Smallwood v. Cromartie* (Nos. 99-1864 and 99-1865), the Court will rule on the constitutionality of a 1997 redrawn Twelfth District. The General Assembly tried to avoid some of the irregular features that had led the Court to invalidate the district in *Shaw v. Reno*, but a three-judge federal district court found the redrawn district to remain "an impermissible and unconstitutional racial gerrymander."

# C. CAMPAIGNS AND ELECTIONS

Among several other rulings on campaign finance and elections, the Court struck down California's "blanket" primacy, under which voters may pick and choose from among candidates of all parties who are listed on a single ballot, in *California Democratic Party v. Jones* (excerpted below). In its 2000–2001 term the Court will also consider, in *Cook v. Gralike*, a 1996 amendment to Missouri's constitution that directs the state's congressional delegation to work to amend the U.S. Constitution to restrict terms for senators to twelve years and for members of the House of Representatives to six years. Adopted one year after *U.S. Term Limits, Inc. v. Thornton*, 514 U.S. 779 (1995) (see Vol. 1, Ch. 5), which invalidated Arkansas's law on term limits, the Missouri law would require placing the words "Disregarded Voters' Instruction on Term Limits" on the ballot next to the name of an incumbent who failed to support term limits and who runs for reelection. For candidates who are not incumbents and refuse to vow to support term limits, the law requires placing the label "Declined to Pledge to Support Term Limits" next to their names. Donald Gralike, a congressional candidate, challenged the constitutionality of the law, and a federal appellate court ruled that it violates candidates' First Amendment rights and unconstitutionally set new qualifications for members of Congress.

THE DEVELOPMENT OF LAW

Other Rulings on Campaign Finance

| Case | Vote | Ruling |
| --- | --- | --- |
| *Nixon v. Shrink Missouri Government PAC*, 120 S.Ct. 897 (2000) | 6:3 | Reaffirming the basic holding in *Buckley v. Valeo*, 424 U.S. 1 (1976), which upheld a $1,000 cap on donations to |

federal candidates over First Amendment objections, the Court upheld Missouri's $1,075 limit on campaign contributions to candidates for state office. Writing for the Court, Justice Souter ruled that the prevention of corruption and the appearance of corruption was a constitutionally sufficient justification for such campaign contribution limits. Justices Kennedy, Scalia, and Thomas dissented, contending that the majority had abandoned "the rigors of our traditional First Amendment structure" and that its ruling would undermine democracy by encouraging the use of "soft money" contributions to political parties, rather than direct contributions to candidates.

THE DEVELOPMENT OF LAW

Other Rulings on Campaigns and Elections

| Case | Vote | Ruling |
| --- | --- | --- |
| *Rice v. Cayetano*, 120 S.Ct. 1044 (2000) | 7:2 | The Court held that the denial of a citizen's right to vote for trustees of the Office of |

Hawaiian Affairs (OHA) violates the Fifteenth Amendment for voting rights. The OHA administers programs for two subclasses of Hawaiians: "Hawaiians" and "native Hawaiians"; both trace their ancestry back to 1778. Rice, a Hawaiian citizen who lacked the ancestry to be designated as "Hawaiian," applied to vote in OHA trustee elections but was denied permission and sued. Writing for the Court, Justice Kennedy ruled that the ancestry requirements were a proxy for race and as such were forbidden by the Fifteenth Amendment. Justices Stevens and Ginsburg dissented.

## *California Democratic Party v. Jones*
### 120 S.Ct. 2402 (2000)

Until 1996, California political parties held closed primaries in which only registered voters in a party voted on its nominees. In 1996, however, the state adopted an initiative, Proposition 198, to change to "blanket" primaries, under which all persons eligible, even those not affiliated with a party, may vote for any candidate, regardless of the candidate's political affiliation, and voters may pick and choose among different parties' candidates for various offices listed on the same ballot. Washington and Alaska also have blanket primaries, whereas twenty other states have "open" primaries, allowing voters to decide on election day which party primary they want to participate in; twenty-five states have "closed" primaries.

The California Democratic Party and three other major parties—each of which prohibited persons not affiliated with their party from voting in their primaries—challenged the adoption of blanket primaries as a violation of their First Amendment freedom of association. A federal district court rejected their claim, and its decision was affirmed by the Court of Appeals for the Ninth Circuit, whose decision was granted review by the Supreme Court.

The appellate court's decision was reversed in a seven to two decision, with the opinion for the Court delivered by Justice Scalia. Justice Stevens filed a dissenting opinion, which Justice Ginsburg joined.

Justice SCALIA delivered the opinion of the Court.

This case presents the question whether the State of California may, consistent with the First Amendment to the United States Constitution, use a so-called "blanket" primary to determine a political party's nominee for the general election. . . .

We have recognized, of course, that States have a major role to play in structuring and monitoring the election process, including primaries. We have considered it "too plain for argument," for example, that a State may require parties to use the primary format for selecting their nominees, in order to assure that intraparty competition is resolved in a democratic fashion. *American Party of Tex. v. White*, 415 U.S. 767 (1974).

Similarly, in order to avoid burdening the general election ballot with frivolous candidacies, a State may require parties to demonstrate "a significant modicum of support" before allowing their candidates a place on that ballot. Finally, in order to prevent "party raiding"—a process in which dedicated members of one party formally switch to another party to alter the outcome of that party's primary—a State may require party registration a reasonable period of time before a primary election.

What we have not held, however, is that the processes by which political parties select their nominees are, as respondents would have it, wholly public affairs that States may regulate freely. To the contrary, we have continually stressed that when States regulate parties' internal processes they must act within limits imposed by the Constitution. . . .

Representative democracy in any populous unit of governance is unimaginable without the ability of citizens to band together in promoting among the electorate candidates who espouse their political views. The formation of national political parties was almost concurrent with the formation of the Republic itself.

Consistent with this tradition, the Court has recognized that the First Amendment protects "the freedom to join together in furtherance of common political beliefs," which "necessarily presupposes the freedom to identify the people who constitute the association, and to limit the association to those people only." That is to say, a corollary of the right to associate is the right not to associate. " 'Freedom of association would prove an empty guarantee if associations could not limit control over their decisions to those who share the interests and persuasions that underlie the association's being.' " [*Democratic Party of United States v. Wisconsin ex rel. La Follette*, 450 U.S. 107 (1981)].

In no area is the political association's right to exclude more important than in the process of selecting its nominee. That process often determines the party's positions on the most significant public policy issues of the day, and even when those positions are predetermined it is the nominee who becomes the party's ambassador to the general electorate in winning it over to the party's views.

Unsurprisingly, our cases vigorously affirm the special place the First Amendment reserves for, and the special protection it accords, the process by which a political party "select[s] a standard bearer who best represents the party's ideologies and preferences." The moment of choosing the party's nominee, we have said, is "the crucial juncture at which the appeal to common principles may be translated into concerted action, and hence to political power in the community." . . .

California's blanket primary violates the principles set forth in these cases. Proposition 198 forces political parties to associate with—to have their nominees, and hence their positions, determined by—those who, at best, have refused to affiliate with the party, and, at worst, have expressly affiliated with a rival. In this respect, it is qualitatively different from a closed primary. Under that system, even when it is made quite easy for a voter to change his party affiliation the day of the primary, and thus, in some sense, to "cross over," at least he must formally become a member of the party; and once he does so, he is limited to voting for candidates of that party.

The evidence in this case demonstrates that under California's blanket primary system, the prospect of having a party's nominee determined by adherents of an opposing party is far from remote—indeed, it is a clear and present danger. For example, in one 1997 survey of California voters 37 percent of Republicans said that they planned to vote in the 1998 Democratic gubernatorial primary, and 20 percent of Democrats said they planned to vote in the 1998 Republican United States Senate primary. . . . The impact of voting by nonparty members is much greater upon minor parties, such as the Libertarian Party and the Peace and Freedom Party. In the first primaries these parties conducted following California's implementation of Proposition 198, the total votes cast for party candidates in some races was more than double the total number of registered party members. . . .

In sum, Proposition 198 forces petitioners to adulterate their candidate-selection process—the "basic function of a political party"—by opening it up to persons wholly unaffiliated with the party. Such forced association has the likely outcome—indeed, in this case the intended outcome—of changing the parties' message. We can think of no heavier burden on a political party's associational freedom. Proposition 198 is therefore unconstitutional unless it is narrowly tailored to serve a compelling state interest. It is to that question which we now turn.

Respondents proffer seven state interests they claim are compelling. Two of them—producing elected officials who better represent the electorate and expanding candidate debate beyond the scope of partisan concerns—are simply circumlocution for producing nominees and nominee positions other than those the parties would choose if left to their own devices. . . .

Respondents' third asserted compelling interest is that the blanket primary is the only way to ensure that disenfranchised persons enjoy the right to an effective vote. By "disenfranchised," respondents do not mean those who cannot vote; they mean simply independents and members of the minority party in "safe" districts. These persons are disenfranchised, according to respondents, because under a closed primary they are unable to participate in what amounts to the determinative election—the majority party's primary; the only way to ensure they have an "effective" vote is to force the party to open its primary to them. This also appears to be nothing more than reformulation of an asserted state interest we have already rejected—recharacterizing nonparty members' keen desire to participate in selection of the party's nominee as "disenfranchisement" if that desire is not fulfilled. . . .

Respondents' remaining four asserted state interests—promoting fairness, affording voters greater choice, increasing voter participation, and protecting privacy—are not, like the others, automatically out of the running; but neither are they, in the circumstances of this case, compelling. That determination is not to be made in the abstract, by asking whether fairness, privacy, etc., are highly significant values; but rather by asking whether the aspect of fairness, privacy, etc., addressed by the law at issue is highly significant. And for all four of these asserted interests, we find it not to be. . . .

Respondents' legitimate state interests and petitioners' First Amendment rights are not inherently incompatible. To the extent they are in this case, the State of California has made them so by forcing political parties to associate with those who do not share their beliefs. And it has done this at the "crucial juncture" at which party members traditionally find their collective voice and select their spokesman. The burden Proposition 198 places on petitioners' rights of political association is both severe and unnecessary. The judgment for the Court of Appeals for the Ninth Circuit is reversed.

Justice STEVENS, with whom Justice GINSBURG joins as to Part I, dissenting.

I

[T]he Court blurs two distinctions that are critical: (1) the distinction between a private organization's right to define itself and its messages, on the one hand, and the State's right to define the obligations of citizens and organizations performing public functions, on the other; and (2) the distinction between laws that abridge participation in the political process and those that encourage such participation.

When a political party defines the organization and composition of its governing units, when it decides what candidates to endorse, and when it decides whether and how to communicate those endorsements to the public, it is engaged in the kind of private expressive associational activity that the First Amendment protects. . . .

I think it clear—though the point has never been decided by this Court—"that a State may require parties to use the primary format for selecting their nominees." The reason a State may impose this significant restriction on a party's associational freedoms is that both the general election and the primary are quintessential forms of state action. It is because the primary is state action that an organization—whether it calls itself a political party or just a "Jaybird" association—may not deny non-Caucasians the right to participate in the selection of its nominees. *Terry v. Adams*, 345 U.S. 461 (1953); *Smith v. Allwright*, 321 U.S. 649 (1944). The Court is quite right in stating that those cases "do not stand for the proposition that party affairs are [wholly] public affairs, free of First Amendment protections." They do, however, stand for the proposition that primary elections, unlike most "party affairs," are state action. The protections that the First Amendment affords to the "internal processes" of a political party do not encompass a right to exclude nonmembers from voting in a state-required, state-financed primary election.

The so-called "right not to associate" that the Court relies upon, then, is simply inapplicable to participation in a state election. A political party, like any other association, may refuse to allow non-members to participate in the party's decisions when it is conducting its own affairs; California's blanket primary system does not infringe this principle. But an election, unlike a convention or caucus, is a public affair. Although it is true that we have extended First Amendment protection to a party's right to invite independents to participate in its primaries, *Tashjian v. Republican Party of Conn.*, 479 U.S. 208 (1986), neither that case nor any other has held or suggested that the "right not to associate" imposes a limit on the State's power to open up its primary elections to all voters eligible to vote in a general election. In my view, while state rules abridging participation in its elections should be closely scrutinized, the First Amendment does not inhibit the State from acting to broaden voter access to state-run, state-financed elections. When a State acts not to limit democratic participation but to expand the ability of individuals to participate in the democratic process, it is acting not as a foe of the First Amendment but as a friend and ally. . . .

In my view, the First Amendment does not mandate that a putatively private association be granted the power to dictate the organizational structure of state-run, state-financed primary elections. It is not this Court's constitutional function to choose between the competing visions of what makes democracy work—party autonomy and discipline versus progressive inclusion of the entire electorate in the process of selecting their public officials—that are held by the litigants in this case. That choice belongs to the people. *U.S. Term Limits, Inc. v. Thornton*, 514 U.S. 779 (1995). . . .

# VOLUME TWO

# 4

---

# THE NATIONALIZATION
# OF THE
# BILL OF RIGHTS

## B. THE RISE AND RETREAT
## OF THE "DUE PROCESS
## REVOLUTION"

---

### THE DEVELOPMENT OF LAW

### Rulings on Substantive and Procedural Due Process

| Case | Vote | Ruling |
| --- | --- | --- |
| *Chicago v. Morales*, 119 S.Ct. 1849 (1999) | 6:3 | In an opinion for the Court, joined only by a plurality, Justice Stevens held that an |

ordinance prohibiting "criminal street gang members" from loitering in public places was impermissibly vague in defining "loitering" and, therefore, failed to give citizens adequate notice of what was forbidden. Justices Scalia and Thomas issued dissenting opinions; Chief Justice Rehnquist joined the latter's dissent.

| | | |
| --- | --- | --- |
| *Troxel v. Granville*, 120 S.Ct. 2054 (2000) | 6:3 | Reaffirming that the Fourteenth Amendment has a substantive component providing |

ing "heightened protection against governmental interference with certain fundamental rights and liberty interests," including that of parents to make

---

decisions concerning the care of their children, the Court held that Washington's statute allowing "any person" "at any time" to petition for visitation rights infringed on parents' "fundamental right to rear children." Writing for the Court, Justice O'Connor rejected the claims of grandparents to visitation rights to their deceased son's daughters over the objection of their mother and affirmed her fundamental right to rear her children. Justices Souter and Thomas filed concurring opinions, whereas Justices Stevens, Scalia, and Kennedy each filed dissents.

# 5

---

# FREEDOM OF EXPRESSION
# AND ASSOCIATION

## A. JUDICIAL APPROACHES TO THE
## FIRST AMENDMENT

### (2) Judicial Line Drawing: *Ad Hoc* and Definitional Balancing

In *Board of Regents of the University of Wisconsin System v. Southworth* (excerpted below) the Court unanimously upheld mandatory university activity fees over the objections of some students that the money was given to groups and organizations that they deemed offensive, and thus ran afoul of their First Amendment guarantee for freedom of speech.

In its 2000–2001 term the Court will take up a related controversy in two companion cases, *Legal Services Corporation v. Velazquez* and *United States v. Velazquez*. The Legal Services Corporation (LSC) was established in 1974 to provide the poor with basic legal services through grants and local legal aid offices. From the outset, Congress restricted the kinds of advocacy funded, prohibiting the LSC from taking cases involving, for instance, abortion and school desegregation. In 1996, the LSC's governing statute was further amended to permit LSC lawyers to seek welfare benefits for clients but forbid them from challenging the constitutionality of changes in federal and state welfare programs. Attorneys for a woman whose benefits were cut and who had sought aid from the LSC contend that the restriction prohibiting challenges to welfare programs is punitive and an unconstitutional restriction under the First Amendment on the advocacy of particular points of view. The Court of Appeals for the Second Circuit agreed, the LSC and the Clinton administration appealed, and the Court granted review. The LSC and the Clinton administration contend that the Court's ruling in *Rust v. Sullivan*, 500 U.S. 173 (1991) (excerpted in Vol. 2, Ch. 5), allows Congress to subsidize various kinds of expression without violating the First Amendment.

# Board of Regents of the University of Wisconsin System v. Southworth
### 120 S.Ct. 1346 (2000)

The pertinent facts are discussed by Justice Kennedy in his opinion for a unanimous Court. Justice Souter, with whom Justices Stevens and Breyer joined, filed a concurring opinion.

Justice KENNEDY delivered the opinion of the Court.

Respondents are a group of students at the University of Wisconsin. They brought a First Amendment challenge to a mandatory student activity fee imposed by petitioner Board of Regents of the University of Wisconsin and used in part by the University to support student organizations engaging in political or ideological speech. Respondents object to the speech and expression of some of the student organizations. Relying upon our precedents which protect members of unions and bar associations from being required to pay fees used for speech the members find objectionable, both the District Court and the Court of Appeals invalidated the University's student fee program. The University contends that its mandatory student activity fee and the speech which it supports are appropriate to further its educational mission.

We reverse. The First Amendment permits a public university to charge its students an activity fee used to fund a program to facilitate extracurricular student speech if the program is viewpoint neutral. We do not sustain, however, the student referendum mechanism of the University's program, which appears to permit the exaction of fees in violation of the viewpoint neutrality principle. . . .

It seems that since its founding the University has required full-time students enrolled at its Madison campus to pay a nonrefundable activity fee. The fee is segregated from the University's tuition charge. Once collected, the activity fees are deposited by the University into the accounts of the State of Wisconsin. The fees are drawn upon by the University to support various campus services and extracurricular student activities. In the University's view, the activity fees "enhance the educational experience" of its students by "promot[ing] extracurricular activities," "stimulating advocacy and debate on diverse points of view," enabling "participa[tion] in political activity," "promot[ing] student participa[tion] in campus administrative activity," and providing "opportunities to develop social skills," all consistent with the University's mission.

The board of regents classifies the segregated fee into allocable and nonallocable portions. The nonallocable portion approximates 80% of the total fee and covers expenses such as student health services, intramural sports, debt service, and the upkeep and operations of the student union facilities. Respondents did not challenge the purposes to which the University commits the nonallocable portion of the segregated fee.

The allocable portion of the fee supports extracurricular endeavors pursued by the University's registered student organizations or RSO's. To qualify for RSO status students must organize as a not-for-profit group, limit membership primarily to students, and agree to undertake activities related to student life on campus. During the 1995–1996 school year, 623 groups had RSO status on the Madison campus.

RSO's may obtain a portion of the allocable fees in one of three ways. Most do so by seeking funding from the Student Government Activity Fund (SGAF), administered by the ASM [Associated Students of Madison]. SGAF moneys may be issued to support an RSO's operations and events, as well as travel expenses "central to the purpose of the organization." As an alternative, an RSO can apply for funding from the General Student Services Fund (GSSF), administered through the ASM's finance committee. These RSO's included a campus tutoring center, the student radio station, a student environmental group, a gay and bisexual student center, a community legal office, an AIDS support network, a campus women's center, and the Wisconsin Student Public Interest Research Group (WISPIRG). The University acknowledges that, in addition to providing campus services (e.g., tutoring and counseling), the GSSF-funded RSO's engage in political and ideological expression.

A student referendum provides a third means for an RSO to obtain funding. While the record is sparse on this feature of the University's program, the parties inform us that the student body can vote either to approve or to disapprove an assessment for a particular RSO. . . .

It is inevitable that government will adopt and pursue programs and policies within its constitutional powers but which nevertheless are contrary to the profound beliefs and sincere convictions of some of its citizens. The government, as a general rule, may support valid programs and policies by taxes or other exactions binding on protesting parties. Within this broader principle it seems inevitable that funds raised by the government will be spent for speech and other expression to advocate and defend its own policies. See, e.g., *Rust v. Sullivan*, 500 U.S. 173 (1991). The case we decide here, however, does not raise the issue of the government's right, or, to be more specific, the state-controlled University's right, to use its own funds to advance a particular message. The University's whole justification for fostering the challenged expression is that it springs from the initiative of the students, who alone give it purpose and content in the course of their extracurricular endeavors.

The University having disclaimed that the speech is its own, we do not reach the question whether traditional political controls to ensure responsible government action would be sufficient to overcome First Amendment objections and to allow the challenged program under the principle that the government can speak for itself. If the challenged speech here were financed by tuition dollars and the University and its officials were responsible for its content, the case might be evaluated on the premise that the government itself is the speaker. That is not the case before us.

The University of Wisconsin exacts the fee at issue for the sole purpose of facilitating the free and open exchange of ideas by, and among, its students. We conclude the objecting students may insist upon certain safeguards with respect to the expressive activities which they are required to support. Our public forum cases are instructive here by close analogy. This is true even though the student activities fund is not a public forum in the traditional sense of the term and despite the circumstance that those cases most often involve a demand for access, not a claim to be exempt from supporting speech. The standard of viewpoint neutrality found in the public forum cases provides the standard we find controlling. We decide that the viewpoint neutrality requirement of the University program is in general sufficient to protect the rights of the objecting students. The student referendum aspect of the program for funding speech and expressive activities, however, appears to be inconsistent with the viewpoint neutrality requirement.

We must begin by recognizing that the complaining students are being required to pay fees which are subsidies for speech they find objectionable, even offensive. The *Abhood* and *Keller* cases, then, provide the beginning point for our analysis. *Abhood v. Detroit Bd. of Ed.*, 431 U.S. 209 (1977); *Keller v. State Bar of Cal.*, 496 U.S. 1 (1990). While those precedents identify the interests of the protesting students, the means of implementing First Amendment protections adopted in those decisions are neither applicable nor workable in the context of extracurricular student speech at a university.

In *Abhood*, some nonunion public school teachers challenged an agreement requiring them, as a condition of their employment, to pay a service fee equal in amount to union dues. The objecting teachers alleged that the union's use of their fees to engage in political speech violated their freedom of association guaranteed by the First and Fourteenth Amendments. The Court agreed and held that any objecting teacher could "prevent the Union's spending a part of their required service fees to contribute to political candidates and to express political views unrelated to its duties as exclusive bargaining representative." The principles outlined in *Abhood*, provided the foundation for our later decision in *Keller*. There we held that lawyers admitted to practice in California could be required to join a state bar association and to fund activities "germane" to the association's mission of "regulating the legal profession and improving the quality of legal services." The lawyers could not, however, be required to fund the bar association's own political expression.

[However, t]he speech the University seeks to encourage in the program before us is distinguished not by discernible limits but by its vast, unexplored bounds. To insist upon asking what speech is germane would be contrary to the very goal the University seeks to pursue. It is not for the Court to say what is or is not germane to the ideas to be pursued in an institution of higher learning.

Just as the vast extent of permitted expression makes the test of germane speech inappropriate for intervention, so too does it underscore the high potential for intrusion on the First Amendment rights of the objecting students. It is all but inevitable that the fees will result in subsidies to speech which some students find objectionable and offensive to their personal beliefs. If the standard of germane speech is inapplicable, then, it might be argued the remedy is to allow each student to list those causes which he or she will or will not support. If a university decided that its students' First Amendment interests were better protected by some type of optional or refund system it would be free to do so. We decline to impose a system of that sort as a constitutional requirement, however. The restriction could be so disruptive and expensive that the program to support extracurricular speech would be ineffective. The First Amendment does not require the University to put the program at risk. . . .

The University must provide some protection to its students' First Amendment interests, however. The proper measure, and the principal standard of protection for objecting students, we conclude, is the requirement of viewpoint neutrality in the allocation of funding support. Viewpoint neutrality was the obligation to which we gave substance in *Rosenberger v. Rector and Visitors of Univ. of Va.*, 515 U.S. 819 (1995). There the University of Virginia feared that any association with a student newspaper advancing religious viewpoints would violate the Establishment Clause. We rejected the argument, holding that the school's adherence to a rule of viewpoint neutrality in administering its student fee program would prevent "any mistaken impression that the student newspapers speak for the University." . . . There is symmetry then in our holding here and in *Rosenberger*: Viewpoint neutrality is the justification for requiring the student to pay the fee in the first instance and for ensuring the integrity of the program's operation once the funds have been collected. We conclude that the University of Wisconsin may sustain the extracurricular dimensions of its programs by using mandatory student fees with viewpoint neutrality as the operational principle.

The parties have stipulated that the program the University has developed to stimulate extracurricular student expression respects the principle of viewpoint neutrality. If the stipulation is to continue to control the case, the University's program in its basic structure must be found consistent with the First Amendment. . . .

It remains to discuss the referendum aspect of the University's program. While the record is not well developed on the point, it appears that by majority vote of the student body a given RSO may be funded or defunded. It is unclear to us what protection, if any, there is for viewpoint neutrality in this part of the process. To the extent the referendum substitutes majority determinations for viewpoint neutrality it would undermine the constitutional protection the program requires. The whole theory of viewpoint neutrality is that minority views are treated with the same respect as are majority views. Access to a public forum, for instance, does not depend upon majoritarian consent. That principle is controlling here. A remand is necessary and appropriate to resolve this point; and the case in all events must be reexamined in light of the principles we have discussed.

Justice SOUTER, with whom Justice STEVENS and Justice BREYER join, concurring in the judgment.

The majority today validates the University's student activity fee after recognizing a new category of First Amendment interests and a new standard of viewpoint neutrality protection. I agree that the University's scheme is permissible, but do not believe that the Court should take the occasion to impose a cast-iron viewpoint neutrality requirement to uphold it. Instead, I would hold that the First Amendment interest claimed by the student respondents (hereinafter Southworth) here is simply insufficient to merit protection by anything more than the viewpoint neutrality already accorded by the University, and I would go no further.

## B. OBSCENITY, PORNOGRAPHY, AND OFFENSIVE SPEECH

### (1) Obscenity and Pornography

For the second time in a decade, the Court addressed the issue of First Amendment protection for nude dancing. In a 1991 five to four decision in *Barnes v. Glen Theatre, Inc.*, 501 U.S. 560 (1991) (in Vol. 2, Ch. 5), the Court upheld a state law banning public nudity as applied to totally nude dancing. That decision prompted the city of Erie, Pennsylvania, to enact a similar ordinance, which was upheld in *City of Erie v. Pap's A.M.* (excerpted below).

In its 2000–2001 term the Court will consider whether Waukesha, Wisconsin's municipal licensing procedure is constitutional in *City News & Novelty, Inc. v. City of Waukesha* (No. 99-1680). City News & Novelty, an adult-oriented business, applied for a renewal of its license, which was denied because the Waukesha council found that the business had allowed minors to loiter on its premises, failed to maintain an unobstructed view of viewing booths, and permitted patrons to engage in sexual acts inside the booths. City News & Novelty appealed, but the state supreme court affirmed the decision, except for a provision for a public hearing on licensing, which it deemed a prior restraint under the First Amendment. At issue is the application of the doctrine of no prior restraint to procedures for the licensing of adult-oriented businesses.

## City of Erie v. Pap's A.M.
### 120 S.Ct. 1382 (2000)

Following the Supreme Court's ruling in *Barnes v. Glen Theatre, Inc.*, 501 U.S. 560 (1991), that Indiana's law against public nudity could apply to nude dancing in adult clubs and require dancers to wear G-strings and pasties instead of dancing totally nude, the city of Erie, Pennsylvania, enacted an ordinance making it an offense to appear in public in a "state of nudity." Two days after the law went into effect, Pap's A.M., the owner of Kandyland, a club that featured totally nude dancing, sought an injunction against the enforcement of the law. The trial court granted an injunction upon finding the ordinance unconstitutional, but an appellate court reversed. Subsequently, the Pennsylvania Supreme Court overruled that decision, holding that nude dancing was expressive conduct protected by the First Amendment. The state supreme court noted that that was the view of eight members of the Supreme Court in *Barnes*, counting four members in the majority and the four dissenters. But, it also concluded that *Barnes* provided no clear precedent because the Court's decision was five to four and its plurality opinion fragmented the justices with four separate and conflicting opinions. Erie appealed and the Supreme Court granted review.

The Court reversed, and its decision was seven-and-a-half to two-and-a-half. Justice O'Connor delivered the opinion for the Court. Justice Scalia, joined by Justice Thomas, filed a concurring opinion. Justice Souter filed a separate opinion, concurring and dissenting in part. Justice Stevens filed a dissent, which Justice Ginsburg joined.

Justice O'CONNOR announced the judgment of the Court, delivered the opinion of the Court with respect to Parts I and II, and delivered an opinion with respect to Parts III and IV, in which Chief Justice REHNQUIST, Justice KENNEDY, and Justice BREYER join.

### III

Being "in a state of nudity" is not an inherently expressive condition. As we explained in *Barnes* [*v. Glen Theatre, Inc.*, 501 U.S. 560 (1991)], however, nude dancing of the type at issue here is expressive conduct, although we think that it falls only within the outer ambit of the First Amendment's protection.

To determine what level of scrutiny applies to the ordinance at issue here, we must decide "whether the State's regulation is related to the suppression of expression." *Texas v. Johnson*, 491 U.S. 397 (1989). If the governmental purpose in enacting the regulation is unrelated to the suppression of expression, then the regulation need only satisfy the "less stringent" standard from [*United States v.*] *O'Brien* [391 U.S. 367 (1968)] for evaluating restrictions on symbolic speech. If the government interest is related to the content of the expression, however, then the regulation falls outside the scope of the *O'Brien* test and must be justified under a more demanding standard.

In *Barnes*, we analyzed an almost identical statute, holding that Indiana's public nudity ban did not violate the First Amendment, although no five Members of the Court agreed on a single rationale for that conclusion. We now clarify that government restrictions on public nudity such as the ordinance at issue here should be evaluated under the framework set forth in *O'Brien* for content-neutral restrictions on symbolic speech.

The ordinance here, like the statute in *Barnes*, is on its face a general prohibition on public nudity. By its terms, the ordinance regulates conduct alone. It does not target nudity that contains an erotic message; rather, it bans all public nudity, regardless of whether that nudity is accompanied by expressive activity. . . .

As Justice SOUTER noted in *Barnes*, "on its face, the governmental interest in combating prostitution and other criminal activity is not at all inherently related to expression." In that sense, this case is similar to *O'Brien*. O'Brien burned his draft registration card as a public statement of his antiwar views, and he was convicted under a statute making it a crime to knowingly mutilate or destroy such a card. This Court rejected his claim that the statute violated his First Amendment rights, reasoning that the law punished him for the "noncommunicative impact of his conduct, and for nothing else." . . . So too here, the ordinance prohibiting public nudity is aimed at combating crime and other negative secondary effects caused by the presence of adult entertainment establishments like Kandyland and not at suppressing the erotic message conveyed by this type of nude dancing. Put another way, the ordinance does not attempt to regulate the primary effects of the expression, i.e., the effect on the audience of watching nude erotic dancing, but rather the secondary effects, such as the impacts on public health, safety, and welfare, which we have previously recognized are "caused by the presence of even one such" establishment. *Renton v. Playtime Theatres, Inc.*, 475 U.S. 41 (1986). . . .

[E]ven if Erie's public nudity ban has some minimal effect on the erotic message by muting that portion of the expression that occurs when the last stitch is dropped, the dancers at Kandyland and other such establishments are free to perform wearing pasties and G-strings. Any effect on the overall expression is *de minimis*. . . .

We conclude that Erie's asserted interest in combating the negative secondary effects associated with adult entertainment establishments like Kandyland is unrelated to the suppression of the erotic message conveyed by nude dancing. The ordinance prohibiting public nudity is therefore valid if it satisfies the four-factor test from *O'Brien* for evaluating restrictions on symbolic speech.

## IV

Applying that standard here, we conclude that Erie's ordinance is justified under *O'Brien*. The first factor of the *O'Brien* test is whether the government regulation is within the constitutional power of the government to enact. Here, Erie's efforts to protect public health and safety are clearly within the city's police powers. The second factor is whether the regulation furthers an important or substantial government interest. The asserted interests of regulating conduct through a public nudity ban and of combating the harmful secondary effects associated with nude dancing are undeniably important. And in terms of demonstrating that such secondary effects pose a threat, the city need not "conduct new studies or produce evidence independent of that already generated by other cities" to demonstrate the problem of secondary effects, "so long as whatever evidence the city relies upon is reasonably believed to be relevant to the problem that the city addresses." *Renton v. Playtime Theatres, Inc.* Because the nude dancing at Kandyland is of the same character as the adult entertainment at issue in *Renton, Young v. American Mini Theatres, Inc.*, 427 U.S. 50 (1976), and *California v. LaRue*, 409 U.S. 109 (1972), it was reasonable for Erie to conclude that such nude dancing was likely to produce the same secondary effects. . . .

In any event, Erie also relied on its own findings. The preamble to the ordinance states that "the Council of the City of Erie has, at various times over more than a century, expressed its findings that certain lewd, immoral activities carried on in public places for profit are highly detrimental to the public health, safety and welfare, and lead to the debasement of both women and men, promote violence, public intoxication, prostitution and other serious criminal activity." The city council members, familiar with commercial downtown Erie, are the individuals who would likely have had first-hand knowledge of what took place at and around nude dancing establishments in Erie, and can make particularized, expert judgments about the resulting harmful secondary effects. Here, Kandyland has had ample opportunity to contest the council's findings about secondary effects—before the council itself, throughout the state proceedings, and before this Court. Yet to this day, Kandyland has never challenged the city council's findings or cast any specific doubt on the validity of those findings. . . .

The ordinance also satisfies *O'Brien*'s third factor, that the government interest is unrelated to the suppression of free expression. The fourth and final *O'Brien* factor—that the restriction is no greater than is essential to the furtherance of the government interest—is satisfied as well. The ordinance regulates conduct, and any incidental impact on the expressive element of nude dancing is *di minimis*. The requirement that dancers wear pasties and G-strings is a minimal restriction in furtherance of the asserted government interests, and the restriction leaves ample capacity to convey the dancer's erotic message. Justice SOUTER points out that zoning is an alternative means of addressing this problem. It is far from clear, however, that zoning imposes less of a burden on expression than the minimal requirement implemented here. In any event, since this is a content-neutral restriction, least restrictive means analysis is not required.

We hold, therefore, that Erie's ordinance is a content-neutral regulation that is valid under *O'Brien*. Accordingly, the judgment of the Pennsylvania Supreme Court is reversed, and the case is remanded for further proceedings not inconsistent with this opinion.


Justice SCALIA, with whom Justice THOMAS joins, concurring in the judgment.

I agree that the decision of the Pennsylvania Supreme Court must be reversed, but disagree with the mode of analysis the Court has applied.

The city of Erie self-consciously modeled its ordinance on the public nudity statute we upheld against constitutional challenge in *Barnes v. Glen Theatre, Inc.*, calculating (one would have supposed reasonably) that the courts of Pennsylvania would consider themselves bound by our judgment on a question of federal constitutional law. In *Barnes*, I voted to uphold the challenged Indiana statute "not because it survives some lower level of First Amendment scrutiny, but because, as a general law regulating conduct and not specifically directed at expression, it is not subject to First Amendment scrutiny at all." Erie's ordinance, too, by its terms prohibits not merely nude dancing, but the act—irrespective of whether it is engaged in for expressive purposes—of going nude in public. The facts that a preamble to the ordinance explains that its purpose, in part, is to "limi[t] a recent increase in nude live entertainment," that city councilmembers in supporting the ordinance commented to that effect, and that the ordinance includes in the definition of nudity the exposure of devices simulating that condition, neither make the law any less general in its reach nor demonstrate that what the municipal authorities really find objectionable is expression rather than public nakedness. As far as appears (and as seems overwhelmingly likely), the preamble, the council members' comments, and the chosen definition of the prohibited conduct simply reflect the fact that Erie had recently been having a public nudity problem not with streakers, sunbathers or hot-dog vendors, but with lap dancers. . . .

Moreover, even were I to conclude that the city of Erie had specifically singled out the activity of nude dancing, I still would not find that this regulation violated the First Amendment unless I could be persuaded (as on this record I cannot) that it was the communicative character of nude dancing that prompted the ban. When conduct other than speech itself is regulated, it is my view that the First Amendment is violated only "[w]here the government prohibits conduct precisely because of its communicative attributes." Here, even if one hypothesizes that the city's object was to suppress only nude dancing, that would not establish an intent to suppress what (if anything) nude dancing communicates. I do not feel the need, as the Court does, to identify some "secondary effects" associated with nude dancing that the city could properly seek to eliminate. (I am highly skeptical, to tell the truth, that the addition of pasties and g-strings will at all reduce the tendency of establishments such as Kandyland to attract crime and prostitution, and hence to foster sexually transmitted disease.) The traditional power of government to foster good morals (bonos mores), and the acceptability of the traditional judgment (if Erie wishes to endorse it) that nude public dancing itself is immoral, have not been repealed by the First Amendment.

Justice SOUTER, concurring in part and dissenting in part.

Erie's stated interest in combating the secondary effects associated with nude dancing establishments is an interest unrelated to the suppression of expression under *United States v. O'Brien*, and the city's regulation is thus properly considered under the *O'Brien* standards. I do not believe, however, that the current record allows us to say that the city has made a sufficient evidentiary showing to sustain its regulation, and I would therefore vacate the decision of the Pennsylvania Supreme Court and remand the case for further proceedings. . . .

[T]he record before us today is deficient in its failure to reveal any evidence on which Erie may have relied, either for the seriousness of the threatened harm or for the efficacy of its chosen remedy. The plurality does the best it can with the materials to hand, but the pickings are slim. . . .

There is one point, however, on which an evidentiary record is not quite so hard to find, but it hurts, not helps, the city. The final *O'Brien* requirement is that the incidental speech restriction be shown to be no greater than essential to achieve the government's legitimate purpose. To deal with this issue, we have to ask what basis there is to think that the city would be unsuccessful in countering any secondary effects by the significantly lesser restriction of zoning to control the location of nude dancing, thus allowing for efficient law enforcement, restricting effects on property values, and limiting exposure of the public. The record shows that for 23 years there has been a zoning ordinance on the books to regulate the location of establishments like Kandyland, but the city has not enforced it. One councilor remarked that "I think there's one of the problems. The ordinances are on the books and not enforced. Now this takes place. You really didn't need any other ordinances." Another commented, "I felt very, very strongly, and I feel just as strongly right now, that this is a zoning matter." Even on the plurality's view of the evidentiary burden, this hurdle to the application of *O'Brien* requires an evidentiary response.

The record suggests that Erie simply did not try to create a record of the sort we have held necessary in other cases, and the suggestion is confirmed by the course of this litigation. The evidentiary question was never decided (or, apparently, argued) below, nor was the issue fairly joined before this Court. . . .

Accordingly, although I join with the plurality in adopting the *O'Brien* test, I respectfully dissent from the Court's disposition of the case.


Justice STEVENS, with whom Justice GINSBURG joins, dissenting.

Far more important than the question whether nude dancing is entitled to the protection of the First Amendment are the dramatic changes in legal doctrine that the Court endorses today. Until now, the "secondary effects" of commercial enterprises featuring indecent entertainment have justified only the regulation of their location. For the first time, the Court has now held that such effects may justify the total suppression of protected speech. Indeed, the plurality opinion concludes that admittedly trivial advancements of a State's interests may provide the basis for censorship. The Court's commendable attempt to replace the fractured decision in *Barnes v. Glen Theatre, Inc.*, with a single coherent rationale is strikingly unsuccessful; it is supported neither by precedent nor by persuasive reasoning.

The Court relies on the so-called "secondary effects" test to defend the ordinance. The present use of that rationale, however, finds no support whatsoever in our precedents. Never before have we approved the use of that doctrine to justify a total ban on protected First Amendment expression. On the contrary, we have been quite clear that the doctrine would not support that end.

In *Young v. American Mini Theatres, Inc.*, 427 U.S. 50 (1976), we upheld a Detroit zoning ordinance that placed special restrictions on the location of motion picture theaters that exhibited "adult" movies. The "secondary effects" of the adult theaters on the neighborhoods where they were located—lower property values and increases in crime (especially prostitution) to name a few—justified the burden imposed by the ordinance. Essential to our holding, however, was the fact that the ordinance was "nothing more than a limitation on the place where adult films may be exhibited" and did not limit the size of the market in such speech.

In *Renton v. Playtime Theatres, Inc.*, 475 U.S. 41 (1986), we upheld a similar ordinance, again finding that the "secondary effects of such theaters on the surrounding community" justified a restrictive zoning law. We noted, however, that "[t]he Renton ordinance, like the one in *American Mini Theatres*, does not ban adult theaters altogether," but merely "circumscribe[s] their choice as to location." Indeed, in both *Renton* and *American Mini Theatres*, the zoning ordinances were analyzed as mere "time, place, and manner" regulations. Because time, place, and manner regulations must "leave open ample alternative channels for communication of information," *Ward v. Rock Against Racism*, 491 U.S. 781 (1989), a total ban would necessarily fail that test. . . .

The reason we have limited our secondary effects cases to zoning and declined to extend their reasoning to total bans is clear and straightforward: A dispersal that simply limits the places where speech may occur is a minimal imposition whereas a total ban is the most exacting of restrictions. The State's interest in fighting presumed secondary effects is sufficiently strong to justify the former, but far too weak to support the latter, more severe burden. . . . The fact that this censorship may have a laudable ulterior purpose cannot mean that censorship is not censorship. For these reasons, the Court's holding rejects the explicit reasoning in *American Mini Theatres* and *Renton*. . . .

The Court's mishandling of our secondary effects cases is not limited to its approval of a total ban. It compounds that error by dramatically reducing the degree to which the State's interest must be furthered by the restriction imposed on speech, and by ignoring the critical difference between secondary effects caused by speech and the incidental effects on speech that may be caused by a regulation of conduct.

In what can most delicately be characterized as an enormous understatement, the plurality concedes that "requiring dancers to wear pasties and G-strings may not greatly reduce these secondary effects." To believe that the mandatory addition of pasties and a G-string will have any kind of noticeable impact on secondary effects requires nothing short of a titanic surrender to the implausible. . . .

Of course, the line between governmental interests aimed at conduct and unrelated to speech, on the one hand, and interests arising out of the effects of the speech, on the other, may be somewhat imprecise in some cases. In this case, however, we need not wrestle with any such difficulty because Erie has expressly justified its ordinance with reference to secondary effects. Indeed, if Erie's concern with the effects of the message were unrelated to the message itself, it is strange that the only means used to combat those effects is the suppression of the message. For these reasons, the Court's argument that "this case is similar to *O'Brien*" is quite wrong. . . . The Court cannot have its cake and eat it too— either Erie's ordinance was not aimed at speech and the Court may attempt to justify the regulation under the incidental burdens test, or Erie has aimed its law at the secondary effects of speech, and the Court can try to justify the law under that doctrine. But it cannot conflate the two with the expectation that Erie's interests aimed at secondary effects will be rendered unrelated to speech by virtue of this doctrinal polyglot. . . .

The censorial purpose of Erie's ordinance precludes reliance on the judgment in *Barnes* as sufficient support for the Court's holding today. Several differences between the Erie ordinance and the statute at issue in Barnes belie the Court's assertion that the two laws are "almost identical." . . . To begin with, the preamble to Erie's ordinance candidly articulates its agenda, declaring: "Council specifically wishes to adopt the concept of Public Indecency prohibited by the laws of the State of Indiana, which was approved by the U.S. Supreme Court in *Barnes v. Glen Theatre Inc.*, for the purpose of limiting a recent increase in nude live entertainment within the City." . . .

It is clear beyond a shadow of a doubt that the Erie ordinance was a response to a more specific concern than nudity in general, namely, nude dancing of the sort found in Kandyland. Given that the Court has not even tried to defend the ordinance's total ban on the ground that its censorship of protected speech might be justified by an overriding state interest, it should conclude that the ordinance is patently invalid. For these reasons, as well as the reasons set forth in Justice WHITE's dissent in *Barnes*, I respectfully dissent.

## (2) Fighting Words and Offensive Speech

In *Wisconsin v. Mitchell*, 508 U.S. 476 (1993) (see Vol. 2, Ch. 5), the Court upheld "hate speech" laws that permit enhanced prison sentences for those convicted of crimes who intentionally selected their victims because of their "race, religion, color, disability, sexual orientation, national origin or ancestry." In *Apprendi v. New Jersey*, 120 S.Ct. 2348 (2000), however, the Court struck down New Jersey's law permitting judges to hand down longer sentences for "hate crimes" based on the "preponderance of evidence" standard. A bare majority ruled that enhanced sentences may only be imposed by a jury and on the basis of the strict "beyond a reasonable doubt" standard. Writing for the Court, Justice Stevens observed that, "other than the fact of prior conviction, any fact that increases the penalty for a crime beyond the prescribed statutory maximum must be submitted to a jury, and proved beyond a reasonable doubt." Writing for dissenting Chief Justice Rehnquist and Justices Breyer and Kennedy, Justice O'Connor criticized the majority for calling into question determinate sentencing and warned that its ruling could "unleash a flood of petitions by convicted defendants seeking to invalidate their sentences."

## D. COMMERCIAL SPEECH

### THE DEVELOPMENT OF LAW

### Other Important Rulings on Commercial Speech and the First Amendment

| Case | Vote | Ruling |
| --- | --- | --- |
| *Greater New Orleans Broadcasting Association v. United States*, 119 S.Ct. 1923 (1999) | 9:0 | In *United States v. Edge Broadcasting Co.*, 509 U.S. 418 (1993) (see Vol. 2, Ch. 5), |

the Court upheld the application of a section of the Communications Act of 1934, forbidding the broadcasting of advertisements for gambling, to bar a radio station in North Carolina, where lotteries are illegal, from broadcasting advertisements for Virginia's lotteries. Here, however, the Court held that the prohibition infringed on First Amendment interests as applied to radio and television broadcasts for private casino gambling in Louisiana, where gambling is legal. Writing for the Court, Justice Stevens emphasized that federal law regulating gambling advertisements is inconsistent and crosscutting. Among the numerous exceptions to the Communications Act's ban on broadcasts for gambling, for instance, Congress in 1975 exempted the broadcasting of advertisements for state-run lotteries and in 1988 exempted the broadcasting of advertisements for gambling operations run by Native American tribes. Because of these exemptions to, and the incoherence of, federal law governing the broadcasting of advertisements for gambling, Justice Stevens held that the government failed to satisfy the four-factor test for regulating commercial speech laid down in *Central Hudson Gas & Electric Corp. v. Public Service Commission of New York*, 447 U.S. 557 (1980) (see Vol. 2, Ch. 5), and reversed the appellate court's decision. Chief Justice Rehnquist and Justice Thomas issued separate concurring opinions.

*Los Angeles Police Department v.*    7:2    Writing for the Court, Chief
*United Reporting Publishing*    Justice Rehnquist upheld a
*Corporation,* 120 S.Ct. 483 (1999)    California law that permits
police departments to give
journalists, scholars, and others access to arrest records, but forbids their
release to companies who would use the information for commercial purposes; the law was enacted to safeguard the privacy of arrestees and victims
and to protect them from solicitations from lawyers and other businesses, as
well as from potential stalkers. The law was challenged by United Reporting
Publishing Corporation, which collects the names and addresses of people
who have been arrested and sells the information to lawyers, insurance companies, and other businesses. It contended that the law ran afoul of the First
Amendment's protection for commercial speech and unconstitutionally discriminated between commercial and noncommercial speech. The U.S. Court
of Appeals for the Ninth Circuit agreed. In reversing the appellate court's
decision, however, Chief Justice Rehnquist ruled that the dispute was less
about free speech concerns than about access to and control over governmental records and information. However, dissenting Justices Stevens and
Kennedy countered that the law unconstitutionally discriminated between
those who may and may not obtain the names and addresses of arrestees and
victims.

## E. FREEDOM OF THE PRESS

In its 2000–2001 term the Court will consider the problem of balancing
individuals' privacy interests in their telephone conversations, and the
reach of federal and state wiretapping laws aimed at preventing people
from intercepting private conversations, versus the First Amendment's protection for the dissemination of information. The companion cases of *Bart-
nicki v. Vopper* and *United States v. Vopper* (Nos. 99-1687 and 99-1728)
stem from heated contract negotiations between the teachers union and the
school board in Wyoming Valley West School District in Pennsylvania. The
president of the union, via her cell phone, angrily told the union's chief
negotiator that if the school board members did not accept its offer, the
teachers were going to "blow off the front porches" of the board members'
homes. An opponent of the union said that he found a recording of the con-
versation in his mailbox and turned it over to a local radio station, which
broadcast it. A divided federal appellate court panel ruled that the application
of wiretapping laws in this case would violate constitutional guarantees for
freedom of speech.

## F. REGULATING THE BROADCAST
## AND CABLE MEDIA, AND THE INTERNET

The Telecommunications Act of 1996 required, in part, cable television operators providing channels "primarily dedicated to sexually-oriented programming" to either fully scramble those channels or limit their transmission to late night hours between 10 P.M. and 6 A.M., when children viewers are unlikely. Scrambling proved imprecise, however, and audio or visual portions of the programs often could be heard or viewed in what is known as "signal bleed." As a result, a majority of the cable operators adopted the "time channeling" approach, which in turn meant that, for two-thirds of the day, no viewers in their service areas could watch sexually oriented programming. That practice was challenged by Playboy Entertainment Group as a content-based restriction in violation of the First Amendment. Writing for the Court, in *United States v. Playboy Entertainment Group, Inc.*, 120 S.Ct. ———— (2000), Justice Kennedy ruled that that section of the Telecommunications Act could not survive strict scrutiny because it was content-based and therefore had to advance a compelling governmental interest in the least restrictive way. Here, Justice Kennedy emphasized the key difference between broadcast television and cable television: Cable television may block unwanted channels on a household-by-household basis, and therefore time channeling on cable television sweeps too broadly. Moreover, he noted that the district court found the government had failed to establish how widespread and serious the problem of signal bleed was for cable viewers. Chief Justice Rehnquist and Justices Breyer, O'Connor, and Scalia dissented.

## H. SYMBOLIC SPEECH AND SPEECH-PLUS-CONDUCT

Returning to the issue of restrictions on antiabortion protesters, dealt with previously in *Madsen v. Women's Health Center*, 512 U.S. 735 (1994), and *Schenck v. Pro-Choice Network of Western New York*, 117 S.Ct. 885 (1997), the Court upheld Colorado's law making it unlawful for a person within 100 feet of a health care facility's entrance to "knowingly approach" within eight feet another person, without permission, in order to pass out leaflets or engage in oral protest. Writing for the Court, in *Hill v. Colorado*, 120 S.Ct. 2480 (2000), Justice Stevens found the statute to be a "narrowly tailored" time, place, and manner regulation, under *Ward v. Rock Against Racism*, 491 U.S. 781 (1989). Justice Scalia, along with Justices Kennedy and Thomas, dissented.

## I. FREEDOM OF ASSOCIATION

In its 1999–2000 term the Court handed down two important rulings on freedom of association. In *California Democratic Party v. Jones* (excerpted above in Vol. 1, ch. 8), the Court struck down California's law permitting "blanket" primaries as a violation of political parties' freedom of association. And in *Boy Scouts of America v. Dale* (excerpted below) a bare majority ruled that the Boy Scouts may exclude homosexuals.

# Boy Scouts of America v. Dale
### 120 S.Ct. 2446 (2000)

Founded in 1910, the Boy Scouts of America is a federally chartered corporation that, as of 1992, included more than 4 million youths and 1 million adults as active members in more than 44,000 Boy Scout troops throughout the country. In 1991 the New Jersey legislature amended its Law Against Discrimination (LAD) to include protection from discrimination based on "affectional or sexual orientation." Subsequently, the Boy Scouts revoked James Dale's Boy Scout Adult membership, upon learning that he was a homosexual, and he sued the Boy Scouts for violating the provisions of LAD.

In 1978, at the age of eight, James Dale joined a Cub Scout Pack and remained a member until 1981, when he became a member of a Boy Scout Troop. He remained a youth member until he reached age 18 in 1988. During that time he earned more than 25 merit badges. In 1989 he sought and received adult membership and became an Assistant Scoutmaster, a position that he held for about a year and a half. About that time, he left home to attend Rutgers University and, while at college, acknowledged for the first time that he was gay. Shortly thereafter Dale became co-president of the Rutgers University Lesbian/Gay Alliance. Then, in July 1990, while attending a seminar on the health needs of lesbian and gay teenagers, Dale was interviewed by the *Star-Ledger*, which subsequently published an article that included Dale's photograph and identified him as the "co-president of the Rutgers University Lesbian/Gay Alliance." Later that month, Dale received from the Boy Scouts a letter revoking his membership and asking him to "sever any relations [he] may have with the Boy Scouts of America." Dale appealed unsuccessfully, and finally, in 1992, he filed a lawsuit in state court against the Boy Scouts of America for discriminating against him in violation of LAD.

The trial court concluded that Dale was "a sexually active homosexual" and the Boy Scouts had always excluded "active homosexual[s]." The court also ruled that the provisions of LAD did not apply to the Boy Scouts because it was not a "public accommodation." A state appellate court reversed and remanded upon concluding that the Boy Scouts were a "public accommodation." The state supreme court affirmed that decision, and the Boy Scouts appealed to the Supreme Court, which granted review.

The decision of the state supreme court was reversed in a five to four decision, and the opinion for the Court was delivered by Chief Justice Rehnquist. Justices Stevens and Souter each filed dissenting opinions, and were joined by Justices Ginsburg and Breyer.

Chief Justice REHNQUIST delivered the opinion of the Court.

In *Roberts v. United States Jaycees*, 468 U.S. 609 (1984), we observed that "implicit in the right to engage in activities protected by the First Amendment" is "a corresponding right to associate with others in pursuit of a wide variety of political, social, economic, educational, religious, and cultural ends." This right is crucial in preventing the majority from imposing its views on groups that would rather express other, perhaps unpopular, ideas. Government actions that may unconstitutionally burden this freedom may take many forms, one of which is "intrusion into the internal structure or affairs of an association" like a "regulation that forces the group to accept members it does not desire." Forcing a group to accept certain members may impair the ability of the group to express those views, and only those views, that it intends to express. Thus, "[f]reedom of association plainly presupposes a freedom not to associate."

The forced inclusion of an unwanted person in a group infringes the group's freedom of expressive association if the presence of that person affects in a significant way the group's ability to advocate public or private viewpoints. *New York State Club Assn., Inc. v. City of New York*, 487 U.S. 1 (1988). But the freedom of expressive association, like many freedoms, is not absolute. We have held that the freedom could be overridden "by regulations adopted to serve compelling state interests, unrelated to the suppression of ideas, that cannot be achieved through means significantly less restrictive of associational freedoms." *Roberts.*

To determine whether a group is protected by the First Amendment's expressive associational right, we must determine whether the group engages in "expressive association." The First Amendment's protection of expressive association is not reserved for advocacy groups. But to come within its ambit, a group must engage in some form of expression, whether it be public or private.

Because this is a First Amendment case where the ultimate conclusions of law are virtually inseparable from findings of fact, we are obligated to independently review the factual record to ensure that the state court's judgment does not unlawfully intrude on free expression. The record reveals the following. The Boy Scouts is a private, nonprofit organization. According to its mission statement: "It is the mission of the Boy Scouts of America to serve others by helping to instill values in young people and, in other ways, to prepare them to make ethical choices over their lifetime in achieving their full potential." "The values we strive to instill are based on those found in the Scout Oath and Law." . . .

Thus, the general mission of the Boy Scouts is clear: "[T]o instill values in young people." The Boy Scouts seeks to instill these values by having its adult leaders spend time with the youth members, instructing and engaging them in activities like camping, archery, and fishing. During the time spent with the youth members, the scoutmasters and assistant scoutmasters inculcate them with the Boy Scouts' values—both expressly and by example. It seems indisputable that an association that seeks to transmit such a system of values engages in expressive activity.

Given that the Boy Scouts engages in expressive activity, we must determine whether the forced inclusion of Dale as an assistant scoutmaster would significantly affect the Boy Scouts' ability to advocate public or private viewpoints. This inquiry necessarily requires us first to explore, to a limited extent, the nature of the Boy Scouts' view of homosexuality.

The values the Boy Scouts seeks to instill are "based on" those listed in the Scout Oath and Law. The Boy Scouts explains that the Scout Oath and Law provide "a positive moral code for living; they are a list of do's rather than don'ts." The Boy Scouts asserts that homosexual conduct is inconsistent with the values embodied in the Scout Oath and Law, particularly with the values represented by the terms "morally straight" and "clean."

Obviously, the Scout Oath and Law do not expressly mention sexuality or sexual orientation. And the terms "morally straight" and "clean" are by no means self-defining. Different people would attribute to those terms very different meanings. For example, some people may believe that engaging in homosexual conduct is not at odds with being "morally straight" and "clean." And others may believe that engaging in homosexual conduct is contrary to being "morally straight" and "clean." The Boy Scouts says it falls within the latter category. . . .

The Boy Scouts asserts that it "teach[es] that homosexual conduct is not morally straight," Brief for Petitioners, and that it does "not want to promote homosexual conduct as a legitimate form of behavior." We accept the Boy Scouts' assertion. We need not inquire further to determine the nature of the Boy Scouts' expression with respect to homosexuality. . . .

The Boy Scouts publicly expressed its views with respect to homosexual conduct by its assertions in prior litigation. For example, throughout a California case with similar facts filed in the early 1980's, the Boy Scouts consistently asserted the same position with respect to homosexuality that it asserts today. We cannot doubt that the Boy Scouts sincerely holds this view.

We must then determine whether Dale's presence as an assistant scoutmaster would significantly burden the Boy Scouts' desire to not "promote homosexual conduct as a legitimate form of behavior." As we give deference to an association's assertions regarding the nature of its expression, we must also give deference to an association's view of what would impair its expression. That is not to say that an expressive association can erect a shield against antidiscrimination laws simply by asserting that mere acceptance of a member from a particular group would impair its message. But here Dale, by his own admission, is one of a group of gay Scouts who have "become leaders in their community and are open and honest about their sexual orientation." Dale was the copresident of a gay and lesbian organization at college and remains a gay rights activist. Dale's presence in the Boy Scouts would, at the very least, force the organization to send a message, both to the youth members and the world, that the Boy Scouts accepts homosexual conduct as a legitimate form of behavior.

*Hurley* [v. *Irish-American Gay, Lesbian, and Bisexual Group of Boston*, 515 U.S. 557 (1995)], is illustrative on this point. There we considered whether the application of Massachusetts' public accommodations law to require the organizers of a private St. Patrick's Day parade to include among the marchers an Irish-American gay, lesbian, and bisexual group, GLIB, violated the parade organizers' First Amendment rights. We noted that the parade organizers did not wish to exclude the GLIB members because of their sexual orientations, but because they wanted to march behind a GLIB banner. We observed: "[A] contingent marching behind the organization's banner would at least bear witness to the fact that some Irish are gay, lesbian, or bisexual, and the presence of the organized marchers would suggest their view that people of their sexual orientations have as much claim to unqualified social acceptance as heterosexuals. The parade's organizers may not believe these facts about Irish sexuality to be so, or they may object to unqualified social acceptance of gays and lesbians or have some other reason for wishing to keep GLIB's message out of the parade. But whatever the reason, it boils down to the choice of a speaker not to propound a particular point of view, and that choice is presumed to lie beyond the government's power to control." Here, we have found that the Boy Scouts believes that homosexual conduct is inconsistent with the values it seeks to instill in its youth members; it will not "promote homosexual conduct as a legitimate form of behavior." As the presence of GLIB in Boston's St. Patrick's Day parade would have interfered with the parade organizers' choice not to propound a particular point of view, the presence of Dale as an assistant scoutmaster would just as surely interfere with the Boy Scout's choice not to propound a point of view contrary to its beliefs. . . .

Having determined that the Boy Scouts is an expressive association and that the forced inclusion of Dale would significantly affect its expression, we inquire whether the application of New Jersey's public accommodations law to require that the Boy Scouts accept Dale as an assistant scoutmaster runs afoul of the Scouts' freedom of expressive association. We conclude that it does.

State public accommodations laws were originally enacted to prevent discrimination in traditional places of public accommodation—like inns and trains. Many on the list are what one would expect to be places where the public is invited. For example, the statute includes as places of public accommodation taverns, restaurants, retail shops, and public libraries. But the statute also includes places that often may not carry with them open invitations to the public, like summer camps and roof gardens. In this case, the New Jersey Supreme Court went a step further and applied its public accommodations law to a private entity without even attempting to tie the term "place" to a physical location. As the definition of "public accommodation" has expanded from clearly commercial entities, such as restaurants, bars, and hotels, to membership organizations such as the Boy Scouts, the potential for conflict between state public accommodations laws and the First Amendment rights of organizations has increased.

We recognized in cases such as *Roberts* and *Duarte* that States have a compelling interest in eliminating discrimination against women in public accommodations. But in each of these cases we went on to conclude that the enforcement of these statutes would not materially interfere with the ideas that the organization sought to express. In *Roberts*, we said "[i]ndeed, the Jaycees has failed to demonstrate any serious burden on the male members' freedom of expressive association." We thereupon concluded in each of these cases that the organizations' First Amendment rights were not violated by the application of the States' public accommodations laws.

In *Hurley*, we said that public accommodations laws "are well within the State's usual power to enact when a legislature has reason to believe that a given group is the target of discrimination, and they do not, as a general matter, violate the First or Fourteenth Amendments." But we went on to note that in that case "the Massachusetts [public accommodations] law has been applied in a peculiar way" because "any contingent of protected individuals with a message would have the right to participate in petitioners' speech, so that the communication produced by the private organizers would be shaped by all those protected by the law who wish to join in with some expressive demonstration of their own." And in the associational freedom cases such as *Roberts*, *Duarte*, and *New York State Club Assn.*, after finding a compelling state interest, the Court went on to examine whether or not the application of the state law would impose any "serious burden" on the organization's rights of expressive association. So in these cases, the associational interest in freedom of expression has been set on one side of the scale, and the State's interest on the other. . . .

The judgment of the New Jersey Supreme Court is reversed, and the cause remanded for further proceedings not inconsistent with this opinion.

Justice STEVENS, with whom Justice SOUTER, Justice GINSBURG, and Justice BREYER join, dissenting.

The majority holds that New Jersey's law violates BSA's right to associate and its right to free speech. But that law does not "impos[e] any serious burdens" on BSA's "collective effort on behalf of [its] shared goals," *Roberts v. United States Jaycees*, 468 U.S. 609 (1984), nor does it force BSA to communicate any message that it does not wish to endorse. New Jersey's law, therefore, abridges no constitutional right of the Boy Scouts. . . .

In light of BSA's self-proclaimed ecumenism, furthermore, it is even more difficult to discern any shared goals or common moral stance on homosexuality. Insofar as religious matters are concerned, BSA's bylaws state that it is "absolutely nonsectarian in its attitude toward religious training." "The BSA does not define what constitutes duty to God or the practice of religion. This is the responsibility of parents and religious leaders." In fact, many diverse religious organizations sponsor local Boy Scout troops. Because a number of religious groups do not view homosexuality as immoral or wrong and reject discrimination against homosexuals, it is exceedingly difficult to believe that BSA nonetheless adopts a single particular religious or moral philosophy when it comes to sexual orientation. This is especially so in light of the fact that Scouts are advised to seek guidance on sexual matters from their religious leaders (and Scoutmasters are told to refer Scouts to them); BSA surely is aware that some religions do not teach that homosexuality is wrong.

The Court seeks to fill the void by pointing to a statement of "policies and procedures relating to homosexuality and Scouting" signed by BSA's President and Chief Scout Executive in 1978 and addressed to the members of the Executive Committee of the national organization. [However, four] aspects of the 1978 policy statement are relevant to the proper disposition of this case. First, at most this letter simply adopts an exclusionary membership policy. But simply adopting such a policy has never been considered sufficient, by itself, to prevail on a right to associate claim.

Second, the 1978 policy was never publicly expressed—unlike, for example, the Scout's duty to be "obedient." It was an internal memorandum, never circulated beyond the few members of BSA's Executive Committee. It remained, in effect, a secret Boy Scouts policy. Far from claiming any intent to express an idea that would be burdened by the presence of homosexuals, BSA's public posture—to the world and to the Scouts themselves—remained what it had always been: one of tolerance, welcoming all classes of boys and young men. In this respect, BSA's claim is even weaker than those we have rejected in the past.

Third, it is apparent that the draftsmen of the policy statement foresaw the possibility that laws against discrimination might one day be amended to protect homosexuals from employment discrimination. Their statement clearly provided that, in the event such a law conflicted with their policy, a Scout's duty to be "obedient" and "obe[y] the laws," even if "he thinks [the laws] are unfair" would prevail in such a contingency. In 1978, however, BSA apparently did not consider it to be a serious possibility that a State might one day characterize the Scouts as a "place of public accommodation" with a duty to open its membership to all qualified individuals. The portions of the statement dealing with membership simply assume that membership in the Scouts is a "privilege" that BSA is free to grant or to withhold. The statement does not address the question whether the publicly proclaimed duty to obey the law should prevail over the private discriminatory policy if, and when, a conflict between the two should arise—as it now has in New Jersey. At the very least, then, the statement reflects no unequivocal view on homosexuality. Indeed, the statement suggests that an appropriate way for BSA to preserve its unpublished exclusionary policy would include an open and forthright attempt to seek an amendment of New Jersey's statute.

Fourth, the 1978 statement simply says that homosexuality is not "appropriate." It makes no effort to connect that statement to a shared goal or expressive activity of the Boy Scouts. Whatever values BSA seeks to instill in Scouts, the idea that homosexuality is not "appropriate" appears entirely unconnected to, and is mentioned nowhere in, the myriad of publicly declared values and creeds of the BSA. That idea does not appear to be among any of the principles actually taught to Scouts. Rather, the 1978 policy appears to be no more than a private statement of a few BSA executives that the organization wishes to exclude gays—and that wish has nothing to do with any expression BSA actually engages in.

The majority also relies on four other policy statements that were issued between 1991 and 1993. All of them were written and issued after BSA revoked Dale's membership. Accordingly, they have little, if any, relevance to the legal question before this Court. In any event, they do not bolster BSA's claim. . . .

It is clear, then, that nothing in these policy statements supports BSA's claim. The only policy written before the revocation of Dale's membership was an equivocal, undisclosed statement that evidences no connection between the group's discriminatory intentions and its expressive interests. The later policies demonstrate a brief—though ultimately abandoned—attempt to tie BSA's exclusion to its expression, but other than a single sentence, BSA fails to show that it ever taught Scouts that homosexuality is not "morally straight" or "clean," or that such a view was part of the group's collective efforts to foster a belief. Furthermore, BSA's policy statements fail to establish any clear, consistent, and unequivocal position on homosexuality. . . .

BSA's claim finds no support in our cases. We have recognized "a right to associate for the purpose of engaging in those activities protected by the First Amendment—speech, assembly, petition for the redress of grievances, and the exercise of religion." *Roberts.* And we have acknowledged that "when the State interferes with individuals' selection of those with whom they wish to join in a common endeavor, freedom of association may be implicated." But "[t]he right to associate for expressive purposes is not absolute"; rather, "the nature and degree of constitutional protection afforded freedom of association may vary depending on the extent to which the constitutionally protected liberty is at stake in a given case." Indeed, the right to associate does not mean "that in every setting in which individuals exercise some discrimination in choosing associates, their selective process of inclusion and exclusion is protected by the Constitution." *New York State Club Assn., Inc. v. City of New York*, 487 U.S. 1 (1988). For example, we have routinely and easily rejected assertions of this right by expressive organizations with discriminatory membership policies, such as private schools, law firms, and labor organizations. In fact, until today, we have never once found a claimed right to associate in the selection of members to prevail in the face of a State's antidiscrimination law. To the contrary, we have squarely held that a State's antidiscrimination law does not violate a group's right to associate simply because the law conflicts with that group's exclusionary membership policy.

In *Roberts v. United States Jaycees*, 468 U.S. 609 (1984), we addressed just such a conflict. The Jaycees was a nonprofit membership organization "designed to inculcate in the individual membership . . . a spirit of genuine Americanism and civic interest, and . . . to provide an avenue for intelligent participation by young men in the affairs of their community." The organization was divided into local chapters, described as "young men's organization[s]," in which regular membership was restricted to males between the ages of 18 and 35. But Minnesota's Human Rights Act, which applied to the Jaycees, made it unlawful to "deny any person the full and equal enjoyment of a place of public accommodation because of sex." The Jaycees, however, claimed that applying the law to it violated its right to associate—in particular its right to maintain its selective membership policy.

We rejected that claim. Cautioning that the right to associate is not "absolute," we held that "[i]nfringements on that right may be justified by regulations adopted to serve compelling state interests, unrelated to the suppression of ideas, that cannot be achieved through means significantly less restrictive of associational freedoms." We found the State's purpose of eliminating discrimination is a compelling state interest that is unrelated to the suppression of ideas. We also held that Minnesota's law is the least restrictive means of achieving that interest. The Jaycees had "failed to demonstrate that the Act imposes any serious burdens on the male members' freedom of expressive association." Though the Jaycees had "taken public positions on a number of diverse issues, [and] regularly engage in a variety of activities worthy of constitutional protection under the First Amendment," there was "no basis in the record for concluding that admission of women as full voting members will impede the organization's ability to engage in these protected activities or to disseminate its preferred views." "The Act," we held, "requires no change in the Jaycees' creed of promoting the interest of young men, and it imposes no restrictions on the organization's ability to exclude individuals with ideologies or philosophies different from those of its existing members."

We took a similar approach in *Board of Directors of Rotary Int'l v. Rotary Club of Duarte*, 481 U.S. 537 (1987). . . .

Several principles are made perfectly clear by *Jaycees* and *Rotary Club*. First, to prevail on a claim of expressive association in the face of a State's antidiscrimination law, it is not enough simply to engage in some kind of expressive activity. Both the Jaycees and the Rotary Club engaged in expressive activity protected by the First Amendment, yet that fact was not dispositive. Second, it is not enough to adopt an openly avowed exclusionary membership policy. Both the Jaycees and the Rotary Club did that as well. Third, it is not sufficient merely to articulate some connection between the group's expressive activities and its exclusionary policy. The Rotary Club, for example, justified its male-only membership policy by pointing to the "aspect of fellowship that is enjoyed by the [exclusively] male membership" and by claiming that only with an exclusively male membership could it "operate effectively" in foreign countries.

Rather, in *Jaycees*, we asked whether Minnesota's Human Rights Law requiring the admission of women "impose[d] any serious burdens" on the group's "collective effort on behalf of [its] shared goals." Notwithstanding the group's obvious publicly stated exclusionary policy, we did not view the inclusion of women as a "serious burden" on the Jaycees' ability to engage in the protected speech of its choice. . . .The relevant question is whether the mere inclusion of the person at issue would "impose any serious burden," "affect in any significant way," or be "a substantial restraint upon" the organization's "shared goals," "basic goals," or "collective effort to foster beliefs." Accordingly, it is necessary to examine what, exactly, are BSA's shared goals and the degree to which its expressive activities would be burdened, affected, or restrained by including homosexuals.

The evidence before this Court makes it exceptionally clear that BSA has, at most, simply adopted an exclusionary membership policy and has no shared goal of disapproving of homosexuality. BSA's mission statement and federal charter say nothing on the matter; its official membership policy is silent; its Scout Oath and Law—and accompanying definitions—are devoid of any view on the topic; its guidance for Scouts and Scoutmasters on sexuality declare that such matters are "not construed to be Scouting's proper area," but are the province of a Scout's parents and pastor; and BSA's posture respecting religion tolerates a wide variety of views on the issue of homosexuality. Moreover, there is simply no evidence that BSA otherwise teaches anything in this area, or that it instructs Scouts on matters involving homosexuality in ways not conveyed in the Boy Scout or Scoutmaster Handbooks. In short, Boy Scouts of America is simply silent on homosexuality. There is no shared goal or collective effort to foster a belief about homosexuality at all—let alone one that is significantly burdened by admitting homosexuals. . . .

Equally important is BSA's failure to adopt any clear position on homosexuality. BSA's temporary, though ultimately abandoned, view that homosexuality is incompatible with being "morally straight" and "clean" is a far cry from the clear, unequivocal statement necessary to prevail on its claim. Despite the solitary sentences in the 1991 and 1992 policies, the group continued to disclaim any single religious or moral position as a general matter and actively eschewed teaching any lesson on sexuality. It also continued to define "morally straight" and "clean" in the Boy Scout and Scoutmaster Handbooks without any reference to homosexuality. As noted earlier, nothing in our cases suggests that a group can prevail on a right to expressive association if it, effectively, speaks out of both sides of its mouth. A State's antidiscrimination law does not impose a "serious burden" or a "substantial restraint" upon the group's "shared goals" if the group itself is unable to identify its own stance with any clarity.

The majority . . . finds that BSA in fact "teach[es] that homosexual conduct is not morally straight." This conclusion, remarkably, rests entirely on statements in BSA's briefs. . . . This is an astounding view of the law. I am unaware of any previous instance in which our analysis of the scope of a constitutional right was determined by looking at what a litigant asserts in his or her brief and inquiring no further. It is even more astonishing in the First Amendment area, because, as the majority itself acknowledges, "we are obligated to independently review the factual record." It is an odd form of independent review that consists of deferring entirely to whatever a litigant claims. But the majority insists that our inquiry must be "limited," because "it is not the role of the courts to reject a group's expressed values because they disagree with those values or find them internally inconsistent."

But nothing in our cases calls for this Court to do any such thing. An organization can adopt the message of its choice, and it is not this Court's place to disagree with it. But we must inquire whether the group is, in fact, expressing a message (whatever it may be) and whether that message (if one is expressed) is significantly affected by a State's antidiscrimination law. More critically, that inquiry requires our independent analysis, rather than deference to a group's litigating posture. . . .

The majority's argument relies exclusively on *Hurley v. Irish-American Gay, Lesbian and Bisexual Group of Boston, Inc.*, 515 U.S. 557 (1995). In that case, petitioners John Hurley and the South Boston Allied War Veterans Council ran a privately operated St. Patrick's Day parade. Respondent, an organization known as "GLIB," represented a contingent of gays, lesbians, and bisexuals who sought to march in the petitioners' parade "as a way to express pride in their Irish heritage as openly gay, lesbian, and bisexual individuals." When the parade organizers refused GLIB's admission, GLIB brought suit under Massachusetts' antidiscrimination law. That statute, like New Jersey's law, prohibited discrimination on account of sexual orientation in any place of public accommodation, which the state courts interpreted to include the parade. Petitioners argued that forcing them to include GLIB in their parade would violate their free speech rights.

We agreed. We first pointed out that the St. Patrick's Day parade—like most every parade—is an inherently expressive undertaking. Next, we reaffirmed that the government may not compel anyone to proclaim a belief with which he or she disagrees. We then found that GLIB's marching in the parade would be an expressive act suggesting the view "that people of their sexual orientations have as much claim to unqualified social acceptance as heterosexuals." Finally, we held that GLIB's participation in the parade "would likely be perceived" as the parade organizers' own speech—or at least as a view which they approved—because of a parade organizer's customary control over who marches in the parade. Though *Hurley* has a superficial similarity to the present case, a close inspection reveals a wide gulf between that case and the one before us today. . . .

Dale's inclusion in the Boy Scouts is nothing like the case in *Hurley*. His participation sends no cognizable message to the Scouts or to the world. Unlike GLIB, Dale did not carry a banner or a sign; he did not distribute any fact sheet;

and he expressed no intent to send any message. If there is any kind of message being sent, then, it is by the mere act of joining the Boy Scouts. Such an act does not constitute an instance of symbolic speech under the First Amendment. . . .

Furthermore, it is not likely that BSA would be understood to send any message, either to Scouts or to the world, simply by admitting someone as a member. Over the years, BSA has generously welcomed over 87 million young Americans into its ranks. In 1992 over one million adults were active BSA members. The notion that an organization of that size and enormous prestige implicitly endorses the views that each of those adults may express in a non-Scouting context is simply mind boggling. . . .

Unfavorable opinions about homosexuals "have ancient roots." *Bowers v. Hardwick*, 478 U.S. 186 (1986). Like equally atavistic opinions about certain racial groups, those roots have been nourished by sectarian doctrine. Over the years, however, interaction with real people, rather than mere adherence to traditional ways of thinking about members of unfamiliar classes, have modified those opinions. A few examples: The American Psychiatric Association's and the American Psychological Association's removal of "homosexuality" from their lists of mental disorders; a move toward greater understanding within some religious communities; Justice BLACKMUN's classic opinion in *Bowers*; Georgia's invalidation of the statute upheld in *Bowers*; and New Jersey's enactment of the provision at issue in this case.

That such prejudices are still prevalent and that they have caused serious and tangible harm to countless members of the class New Jersey seeks to protect are established matters of fact that neither the Boy Scouts nor the Court disputes. That harm can only be aggravated by the creation of a constitutional shield for a policy that is itself the product of a habitual way of thinking about strangers. As Justice BRANDEIS so wisely advised, "we must be ever on our guard, lest we erect our prejudices into legal principles."

If we would guide by the light of reason, we must let our minds be bold. I respectfully dissent.

# 6

# FREEDOM FROM
# AND OF RELIGION

## A. THE (DIS)ESTABLISHMENT OF RELIGION

In *Santa Fe Independent School District v. Doe* (excerpted below), the Court extended its ruling in *Lee v. Weisman*, 505 U.S. 577 (1992) (excerpted in Vol. 2, Ch. 6), holding that school-sponsored prayer at graduation ceremonies violates the First Amendment, to invalidate school-sponsored, student-led prayers at football games. However, overruling two precedents in *Mitchell v. Helms* (excerpted below), the Court upheld public school districts' loan of computer software and hardware, as well as other forms of aid, to private religious schools.

## *Santa Fe Independent School District v. Doe*
120 S.Ct. ———— (2000)

Before 1995, at the Santa Fe High School in Texas, an elected student counsel chaplain delivered a prayer over the public address system before each varsity football game. When that practice, along with student-led prayers at graduation ceremonies, was challenged for violating the First Amendment (dis)establishment clause, the school district adopted a new policy—initially entitled "Prayer at Football Games"—permitting, but not requiring, prayer initiated and led by students at all home games. Under this policy, students held two elections: one to determine whether prayers should be delivered before football games and, if so, a second to select the spokesperson to deliver them. A federal district court issued an order, relying on the holding in *Lee v. Weisman*, 505 U.S. 577 (1992), that benedictions at high school graduation ceremonies run afoul of the First Amendment, to preclude student-led prayers at both graduation ceremonies and football games. However, the school district modified its policy to omit the word *prayer* in the title of its policy, referring instead to *messages, statements,* and *invocations*. When that decision was appealed, the Court of Appeals for the Fifth Circuit concluded that the district's policy violated the First Amendment. The school district appealed to the Supreme Court, which granted review.

The appellate court's decision was affirmed by a six to three vote, and Justice Stevens delivered the opinion for the Court. Chief Justice Rehnquist filed a dissenting opinion, joined by Justices Scalia and Thomas.

Justice STEVENS delivered the opinion of the Court.

In *Lee v. Weisman*, 505 U.S. 577 (1992), we held that a prayer delivered by a rabbi at a middle school graduation ceremony violated that Clause. Although this case involves student prayer at a different type of school function, our analysis is properly guided by the principles that we endorsed in *Lee*.

In this case the District first argues that "there is a crucial difference between government speech endorsing religion, which the Establishment Clause forbids, and private speech endorsing religion, which the Free Speech and Free Exercise Clauses protect." *Board of Ed. of Westside Community Schools (Dist. 66) v. Mergens*, 496 U.S. 226 (1990). We certainly agree with that distinction, but we are not persuaded that the pregame invocations should be regarded as "private speech."

These invocations are authorized by a government policy and take place on government property at government-sponsored school-related events. Of course, not every message delivered under such circumstances is the government's own. We have held, for example, that an individual's contribution to a government-created forum was not government speech. See *Rosenberger v. Rector and Visitors of Univ. of Va.*, 515 U.S. 819 (1995). [But, here] the school allows only one student, the same student for the entire season, to give the invocation. The statement or invocation, moreover, is subject to particular regulations that confine the content and topic of the student's message.

Granting only one student access to the stage at a time does not, of course, necessarily preclude a finding that a school has created a limited public forum. Here, however, Santa Fe's student election system ensures that only those messages deemed "appropriate" under the District's policy may be delivered. That is, the majoritarian process implemented by the District guarantees, by definition, that minority candidates will never prevail and that their views will be effectively silenced.

Recently, in *Board of Regents of Univ. of Wis. System v. Southworth*, [120 S.Ct. 1346] (2000), we explained why student elections that determine, by majority vote, which expressive activities shall receive or not receive school benefits are constitutionally problematic. . . . Like the student referendum for funding in *Southworth*, this student election does nothing to protect minority views but rather places the students who hold such views at the mercy of the majority. Because "fundamental rights may not be submitted to vote[,] they depend on the outcome of no elections," *West Virginia Bd. of Ed. v. Barnette*, 319 U.S. 624 (1943), the District's elections are insufficient safeguards of diverse student speech. . . .

Moreover, the District has failed to divorce itself from the religious content in the invocations. . . . The decision whether to deliver a message is first made by majority vote of the entire student body, followed by a choice of the speaker in a separate, similar majority election. Even though the particular words used by the speaker are not determined by those votes, the policy mandates that the "statement or invocation" be "consistent with the goals and purposes of this policy," which are "to solemnize the event, to promote good sportsmanship and student safety, and to establish the appropriate environment for the competition."

In addition to involving the school in the selection of the speaker, the policy, by its terms, invites and encourages religious messages. The policy itself states that the purpose of the message is "to solemnize the event." A religious message is the most obvious method of solemnizing an event. Moreover, the requirements that the message "promote good citizenship" and "establish the appropriate environment for competition" further narrow the types of message deemed appropriate, suggesting that a solemn, yet nonreligious, message, such as commentary on United States foreign policy, would be prohibited. Indeed, the only type of message that is expressly endorsed in the text is an "invocation"—a term that primarily describes an appeal for divine assistance. In fact, as used in the past at Santa Fe High School, an "invocation" has always entailed a focused religious message. Thus, the expressed purposes of the policy encourage the selection of a religious message, and that is precisely how the students understand the policy. The results of the elections described in the parties' stipulation make it clear that the students understood that the central question before them was whether prayer should be a part of the pregame ceremony.

The actual or perceived endorsement of the message, moreover, is established by factors beyond just the text of the policy. Once the student speaker is selected and the message composed, the invocation is then delivered to a large audience assembled as part of a regularly scheduled, school-sponsored function conducted on school property. The message is broadcast over the school's public address system, which remains subject to the control of school officials. It is fair to assume that the pregame ceremony is clothed in the traditional indicia of school sporting events, which generally include not just the team, but also cheerleaders and band members dressed in uniforms sporting the school name and mascot. The school's name is likely written in large print across the field and on banners and flags. The crowd will certainly include many who display the school colors and insignia on their school T-shirts, jackets, or hats and who may also be waving signs displaying the school name. It is in a setting such as this that "[t]he board has chosen to permit" the elected student to rise and give the "statement or invocation."

In this context the members of the listening audience must perceive the pregame message as a public expression of the views of the majority of the student body delivered with the approval of the school administration. In cases involving state participation in a religious activity, one of the relevant questions is "whether an objective observer, acquainted with the text, legislative history, and implementation of the statute, would perceive it as a state endorsement of prayer in public schools." *Wallace* [*v. Jaffree*, 472 U.S. 38 (1985)]. Regardless of the listener's support for, or objection to, the message, an objective Santa Fe High School student will unquestionably perceive the inevitable pregame prayer as stamped with her school's seal of approval.

The District next argues that its football policy is distinguishable from the graduation prayer in *Lee* because it does not coerce students to participate in religious observances. Its argument has two parts: first, that there is no impermissible government coercion because the pregame messages are the product of student choices; and second, that there is really no coercion at all because attendance at an extracurricular event, unlike a graduation ceremony, is voluntary.

The reasons just discussed explaining why the alleged "circuit-breaker" mechanism of the dual elections and student speaker do not turn public speech into private speech also demonstrate why these mechanisms do not insulate the school from the coercive element of the final message. In fact, this aspect of the District's argument exposes anew the concerns that are created by the majoritarian election system. The parties' stipulation clearly states that the issue resolved in the first election was "whether a student would deliver prayer at varsity football games," and the controversy in this case demonstrates that the views of the students are not unanimous on that issue.

One of the purposes served by the Establishment Clause is to remove debate over this kind of issue from governmental supervision or control. We explained in *Lee* that the "preservation and transmission of religious beliefs and worship is a responsibility and a choice committed to the private sphere." The two student elections authorized by the policy, coupled with the debates that presumably must precede each, impermissibly invade that private sphere. . . .

The District further argues that attendance at the commencement ceremonies at issue in *Lee* "differs dramatically" from attendance at high school football games, which it contends "are of no more than passing interest to many students" and are "decidedly extracurricular," thus dissipating any coercion. Attendance at a high school football game, unlike showing up for class, is certainly not required in order to receive a diploma.

There are some students, however, such as cheerleaders, members of the band, and, of course, the team members themselves, for whom seasonal commitments mandate their attendance, sometimes for class credit. The District also minimizes the importance to many students of attending and participating in extracurricular activities as part of a complete educational experience. As we noted in *Lee*, "[l]aw reaches past formalism." To assert that high school students do not feel immense social pressure, or have a truly genuine desire, to be involved in the extracurricular event that is American high school football is "formalistic in the extreme." . . .

Under the *Lemon* [*v. Kurtzman*, 403 U.S. 602 (1971)] standard, a court must invalidate a statute if it lacks "a secular legislative purpose." It is therefore proper, as part of this facial challenge, for us to examine the purpose of the October policy.

As discussed, . . the plain language of the policy clearly spells out the extent of school involvement in both the election of the speaker and the content of the message. Additionally, the text of the October policy specifies only one, clearly preferred message—that of Santa Fe's traditional religious "invocation." Finally, the extremely selective access of the policy and other content restrictions confirm that it is not a content-neutral regulation that creates a limited public forum for the expression of student speech. . . .

The judgment of the Court of Appeals is, accordingly, affirmed. It is so ordered.

Chief Justice REHNQUIST, with whom Justice SCALIA and Justice THOMAS join, dissenting.

The Court distorts existing precedent to conclude that the school district's student-message program is invalid on its face under the Establishment Clause. But even more disturbing than its holding is the tone of the Court's opinion; it bristles with hostility to all things religious in public life. Neither the holding nor the tone of the opinion is faithful to the meaning of the Establishment Clause, when it is recalled that George Washington himself, at the request of the very Congress which passed the Bill of Rights, proclaimed a day of "public thanksgiving and prayer, to be observed by acknowledging with grateful hearts the many and signal favors of Almighty God."

The Court . . . invalidates the district's policy on its face. To do so, it applies the most rigid version of the oft-criticized test of *Lemon v. Kurtzman*, 403 U.S. 602 (1971).

*Lemon* has had a checkered career in the decisional law of this Court. [But, even] if it were appropriate to apply the *Lemon* test here, the district's student-message policy should not be invalidated on its face. The Court applies *Lemon* and holds that the "policy is invalid on its face because it establishes an improper majoritarian election on religion, and unquestionably has the purpose and creates the perception of encouraging the delivery of prayer at a series of important school events." The Court's reliance on each of these conclusions misses the mark.

First, the Court misconstrues the nature of the "majoritarian election" permitted by the policy as being an election on "prayer" and "religion." To the contrary, the election . . . could become one in which student candidates campaign on platforms that focus on whether or not they will pray if elected. It is also conceivable that the election could lead to a Christian prayer before 90 percent of the football games. If, upon implementation, the policy operated in this fashion, we would have a record before us to review whether the policy, as applied, violated the Establishment Clause or unduly suppressed minority viewpoints. But it is possible that the students might vote not to have a pregame speaker, in which case there would be no threat of a constitutional violation. . . .

Second, with respect to the policy's purpose, the Court holds that "the simple enactment of this policy, with the purpose and perception of school endorsement of student prayer, was a constitutional violation." But the policy itself has plausible secular purposes: "[T]o solemnize the event, to promote good sportsmanship and student safety, and to establish the appropriate environment for the competition." Where a governmental body "expresses a plausible secular purpose" for an enactment, "courts should generally defer to that stated intent." *Wallace.*

The Court also relies on our decision in *Lee v. Weisman*, 505 U.S. 577 (1992), to support its conclusion. In *Lee*, we concluded that the content of the speech at issue, a graduation prayer given by a rabbi, was "directed and controlled" by a school official. In other words, at issue in *Lee* was government speech. Here, by contrast, the potential speech at issue, if the policy had been allowed to proceed, would be a message or invocation selected or created by a student. That is, if there were speech at issue here, it would be private speech.

Finally, the Court seems to demand that a government policy be completely neutral as to content or be considered one that endorses religion. This is undoubtedly a new requirement, as our Establishment Clause jurisprudence simply does not mandate "content neutrality." That concept is found in our First Amendment speech cases and is used as a guide for determining when we apply strict scrutiny. For example, we look to "content neutrality" in reviewing loudness restrictions imposed on speech in public forums, see *Ward v. Rock Against Racism*, 491 U.S. 781 (1989), and regulations against picketing, see *Boos v. Barry*, 485 U.S. 312 (1988). The Court seems to think that the fact that the policy is not content neutral somehow controls the Establishment Clause inquiry.

But even our speech jurisprudence would not require that all public school actions with respect to student speech be content neutral. See, e.g., *Bethel School Dist. No. 403 v. Fraser*, 478 U.S. 675 (1986) (allowing the imposition of sanctions against a student speaker who, in nominating a fellow student for elective office during an assembly, referred to his candidate in terms of an elaborate sexually explicit metaphor). Schools do not violate the First Amendment every time they restrict student speech to certain categories. But under the Court's view, a school policy under which the student body president is to solemnize the graduation ceremony by giving a favorable introduction to the guest speaker would be facially unconstitutional. Solemnization "invites and encourages" prayer and the policy's content limitations prohibit the student body president from giving a solemn, yet non-religious, message like "commentary on United States foreign policy."

The policy at issue here may be applied in an unconstitutional manner, but it will be time enough to invalidate it if that is found to be the case. I would reverse the judgment of the Court of Appeals.

## *Mitchell v. Helms*
### 120 S.Ct. 2530 (2000)

In Chapter 2 of the Education Consolidation and Improvement Act of 1981, authorizes federal funds for state and local educational agencies, which in turn lend educational materials and equipment, such as library and media materials, as well as computer software and hardware, to public and private elementary and secondary schools to implement "secular, neutral, and nonideological" programs. In an average year, Jefferson Parish, Louisiana, allocated about 30 percent of its Chapter 2 funds to private schools, most of which are Catholic or otherwise religiously affiliated. That practice was challenged as a violation of the First Amendment (dis)establishment clause. A federal district court agreed, relying on *Meek v. Pittenger*, 421 U.S. 349 (1975), and *Wolman v. Walter*, 433 U.S. 229 (1997), which struck down programs providing many of the same kinds of materials and equipment. But, after the presiding district court judge retired, another judge reversed the decision on the basis of *Zobrest v. Catalina Foothills Schools District*, 509 U.S. 1 (1993), which allowed, under a federal program for the disabled, a public school to provide a sign-language interpreter for a deaf student in a Catholic high school. While that decision was appealed, the Supreme Court handed down *Agostini v. Felton*, 521 U.S. 203

(1997), which approved a program, under Title I of the Elementary and Secondary Education Act of 1965, providing public school teachers for remedial classes at religious and other private schools. Subsequently, in reversing the district court's decision allowing Chapter 2 funds to go to Catholic schools, the Court of Appeals for the Fifth Circuit concluded that the ruling in *Agostini* neither overruled *Meek* and *Wolman*, nor rejected their distinction between loaning textbooks and other kinds of materials and equipment, which might be diverted for religious purposes to private religious schools. That decision was appealed, and the Supreme Court granted review.

The appellate court's decision was reversed in a six to three decision, with opinion for the Court delivered by Justice Thomas. Justice O'Connor filed a concurring opinion. Justice Souter filed a dissenting opinion, which Justices Stevens and Ginsburg joined.

Justice THOMAS announced the judgment of the Court and delivered an opinion, in which the Chief Justice Rehnquist, Justice SCALIA, and Justice KENNEDY join.

The question is whether Chapter 2, as applied in Jefferson Parish, Louisiana, is a law respecting an establishment of religion, because many of the private schools receiving Chapter 2 aid in that parish are religiously affiliated. We hold that Chapter 2 is not such a law.

The Establishment Clause of the First Amendment dictates that "Congress shall make no law respecting an establishment of religion." In the over 50 years since *Everson* [v. *Bd. of Education*, 330 U.S. 1 (1947)], we have consistently struggled to apply these simple words in the context of governmental aid to religious schools.

In *Agostini* [v. *Felton*, 117 S.Ct. 1997 (1997)], however, we brought some clarity to our case law, by overruling two anomalous precedents (one in whole, the other in part) and by consolidating some of our previously disparate considerations under a revised test. Whereas in *Lemon* [v. *Kurtzman*, 403 U.S. 602 (1971)], we had considered whether a statute (1) has a secular purpose, (2) has a primary effect of advancing or inhibiting religion, or (3) creates an excessive entanglement between government and religion, in *Agostini* we modified *Lemon* for purposes of evaluating aid to schools and examined only the first and second factors. We acknowledged that our cases discussing excessive entanglement had applied many of the same considerations as had our cases discussing primary effect, and we therefore recast *Lemon*'s entanglement inquiry as simply one criterion relevant to determining a statute's effect. We also acknowledged that our cases had pared somewhat the factors that could justify a finding of excessive entanglement. We then set out revised criteria for determining the effect of a statute: "To summarize, New York City's Title I program does not run afoul of any of three primary criteria we currently use to evaluate whether government aid has the effect of advancing religion: It does not result in governmental indoctrination; define its recipients by reference to religion; or create an excessive entanglement."

In this case, our inquiry under *Agostini*'s purpose and effect test is a narrow one. Because respondents do not challenge the District Court's holding that Chapter 2 has a secular purpose, and because the Fifth Circuit also did not question that holding, we will consider only Chapter 2's effect. Further, in determining that effect, we will consider only the first two *Agostini* criteria, since neither respondents nor the Fifth Circuit has questioned the District Court's holding that Chapter 2 does not create an excessive entanglement. Considering Chapter 2 in light of our more recent case law, we conclude that it neither results in religious indoctrination by the government nor defines its recipients by reference to religion. We therefore hold that Chapter 2 is not a "law respecting an establishment of religion." In so holding, we acknowledge what both the Ninth and Fifth Circuits saw was inescapable—*Meek* [*v. Pittenger*, 421 U.S. 349 (1975)] and *Wolman* [*v. Walter*, 433 U.S. 229 (1977)], are anomalies in our case law. We therefore conclude that they are no longer good law.

As we indicated in *Agostini*, and have indicated elsewhere, the question whether governmental aid to religious schools results in governmental indoctrination is ultimately a question whether any religious indoctrination that occurs in those schools could reasonably be attributed to governmental action. We have also indicated that the answer to the question of indoctrination will resolve the question whether a program of educational aid "subsidizes" religion, as our religion cases use that term.

In distinguishing between indoctrination that is attributable to the State and indoctrination that is not, we have consistently turned to the principle of neutrality, upholding aid that is offered to a broad range of groups or persons without regard to their religion. If the religious, irreligious, and areligious are all alike eligible for governmental aid, no one would conclude that any indoctrination that any particular recipient conducts has been done at the behest of the government. . . .

As a way of assuring neutrality, we have repeatedly considered whether any governmental aid that goes to a religious institution does so "only as a result of the genuinely independent and private choices of individuals." *Agostini*. We have viewed as significant whether the "private choices of individual parents," as opposed to the "unmediated" will of government, [*School District of Grand Rapids v.*] *Ball*, [473 U.S. 373 (1985)], determine what schools ultimately benefit from the governmental aid, and how much. For if numerous private choices, rather than the single choice of a government, determine the distribution of aid pursuant to neutral eligibility criteria, then a government cannot, or at least cannot easily, grant special favors that might lead to a religious establishment. Private choice also helps guarantee neutrality by mitigating the preference for pre-existing recipients that is arguably inherent in any governmental aid program, and that could lead to a program inadvertently favoring one religion or favoring religious private schools in general over nonreligious ones.

The principles of neutrality and private choice, and their relationship to each other, were prominent not only in *Agostini*, but also in *Zobrest* [*v. Catalina Foothills School District*, 509 U.S. 1 (1993); *Witters* [*v. Washington Dept. of Services for the Blind*, 474 U.S. 481 (1986)]; and *Mueller* [*v. Allen*, 463 U.S. 388 (1983)]. . . .

*Agostini*'s second primary criterion for determining the effect of governmental aid is closely related to the first. The second criterion requires a court to consider whether an aid program "define[s] its recipients by reference to religion." As we briefly explained in *Agostini*, this second criterion looks to the same set of facts as does our focus, under the first criterion, on neutrality, but the second criterion uses those facts to answer a somewhat different question—whether the criteria for allocating the aid "creat[e] a financial incentive to undertake religious indoctrination." In *Agostini* we set out the following rule for answering this question: "This incentive is not present, however, where the aid is allocated on the basis of neutral, secular criteria that neither favor nor disfavor religion, and is made available to both religious and secular beneficiaries on a nondiscriminatory basis. Under such circumstances, the aid is less likely to have the effect of advancing religion." The cases on which *Agostini* relied for this rule, and *Agostini* itself, make clear the close relationship between this rule, incentives, and private choice. For to say that a program does not create an incentive to choose religious schools is to say that the private choice is truly "independent," *Witters.* When such an incentive does exist, there is a greater risk that one could attribute to the government any indoctrination by the religious schools. See *Zobrest.*

We hasten to add, what should be obvious from the rule itself, that simply because an aid program offers private schools, and thus religious schools, a benefit that they did not previously receive does not mean that the program, by reducing the cost of securing a religious education, creates, under *Agostini*'s second criterion, an "incentive" for parents to choose such an education for their children. For any aid will have some such effect. . . .

Respondents also contend that the Establishment Clause requires that aid to religious schools not be impermissibly religious in nature or be divertible to religious use. We agree with the first part of this argument but not the second. Respondents' "no divertibility" rule is inconsistent with our more recent case law and is unworkable. So long as the governmental aid is not itself "unsuitable for use in the public schools because of religious content," *Allen,* and eligibility for aid is determined in a constitutionally permissible manner, any use of that aid to indoctrinate cannot be attributed to the government and is thus not of constitutional concern. And, of course, the use to which the aid is put does not affect the criteria governing the aid's allocation and thus does not create any impermissible incentive under *Agostini*'s second criterion. . . .

Justice O'CONNOR acknowledges that the Court in *Zobrest* and *Witters* approved programs that involved actual diversion. The dissent likewise does not deny that *Witters* involved actual diversion. The dissent does claim that the aid in *Zobrest* "was not considered divertible," but the dissent in *Zobrest,* which the author of today's dissent joined, understood the case otherwise. As that dissent made clear, diversion is the use of government aid to further a religious message. By that definition, the government-provided interpreter in *Zobrest* was not only divertible, but actually diverted.

Respondents appear to rely on *Meek* and *Wolman* to establish their rule against "divertible" aid. But those cases offer little, if any, support for respondents. *Meek* mentioned divertibility only briefly in a concluding footnote, and that mention was, at most, peripheral to the Court's reasoning in striking down the lending of instructional materials and equipment. The aid program in *Wolman* explicitly barred divertible aid, so a concern for divertibility could not have been part of our reason for finding that program invalid. The issue is not divertibility of aid but rather whether the aid itself has an impermissible content. Where the aid would be suitable for use in a public school, it is also suitable for use in any private school. Similarly, the prohibition against the government providing impermissible content resolves the Establishment Clause concerns that exist if aid is actually diverted to religious uses. In *Agostini*, we explained *Zobrest* by making just this distinction between the content of aid and the use of that aid: "Because the only government aid in *Zobrest* was the interpreter, who was herself not inculcating any religious messages, no government indoctrination took place." *Agostini* also acknowledged that what the dissenters in *Zobrest* had charged was essentially true: *Zobrest* did effect a "shift in our Establishment Clause law." The interpreter herself, assuming that she fulfilled her assigned duties, had "no inherent religious significance," *Allen*, and so it did not matter (given the neutrality and private choice involved in the program) that she "would be a mouthpiece for religious instruction." *Agostini*. And just as a government interpreter does not herself inculcate a religious message—even when she is conveying one—so also a government computer or overhead projector does not itself inculcate a religious message, even when it is conveying one.

In *Agostini* itself, we approved the provision of public employees to teach secular remedial classes in private schools partly because we concluded that there was no reason to suspect that indoctrinating content would be part of such governmental aid. Relying on *Zobrest*, we refused to presume that the public teachers would "inject religious content" into their classes, especially given certain safeguards that existed; we also saw no evidence that they had done so. . . .

In short, nothing in the Establishment Clause requires the exclusion of pervasively sectarian schools from otherwise permissible aid programs, and other doctrines of this Court bar it. This doctrine, born of bigotry, should be buried now.

Applying the two relevant *Agostini* criteria, we see no basis for concluding that Jefferson Parish's Chapter 2 program "has the effect of advancing religion." Chapter 2 does not result in governmental indoctrination, because it determines eligibility for aid neutrally, allocates that aid based on the private choices of the parents of schoolchildren, and does not provide aid that has an impermissible content. Nor does Chapter 2 define its recipients by reference to religion. . . .

There is evidence that equipment has been, or at least easily could be, diverted for use in religious classes. Justice O'CONNOR, however, finds the safeguards against diversion adequate to prevent and detect actual diversion. The safeguards on which she relies reduce to three: (1) signed assurances that Chapter 2 aid will be used only for secular, neutral, and nonideological purposes, (2) monitoring visits, and (3) the requirement that equipment be labeled as belonging to Chapter 2. . . . In any event, for reasons we discussed supra, the evidence of actual diversion and the weakness of the safeguards against actual diversion are not relevant to the constitutional inquiry, whatever relevance they may have under the statute and regulations. . . .

Chapter 2 satisfies both the first and second primary criteria of *Agostini*. It therefore does not have the effect of advancing religion. For the same reason, Chapter 2 also "cannot reasonably be viewed as an endorsement of religion." Accordingly, we hold that Chapter 2 is not a law respecting an establishment of religion. Jefferson Parish need not exclude religious schools from its Chapter 2 program. To the extent that *Meek* and *Wolman* conflict with this holding, we overrule them.

Our conclusion regarding *Meek* and *Wolman* should come as no surprise. The Court as early as *Wolman* itself left no doubt that *Meek* and *Allen* were irreconcilable, and we have repeatedly reaffirmed *Allen* since then, see, e.g., *Agostini*.

Less than three years after *Wolman*, we explained that *Meek* did not, despite appearances, hold that "all loans of secular instructional material and equipment inescapably have the effect of direct advancement of religion." [*Committee for Public Education v.*] *Regan*, [444 U.S. 646 (1980)]. Then, in *Mueller*, we conceded that the aid at issue in *Meek* and *Wolman* did "resembl[e], in many respects," the aid that we had upheld in *Everson* and *Allen*. Most recently, *Agostini*, in rejecting *Ball*'s assumption that "all government aid that directly assists the educational function of religious schools is invalid," necessarily rejected a large portion (perhaps all, see *Ball*) of the reasoning of *Meek* and *Wolman* in invalidating the lending of materials and equipment, for *Ball* borrowed that assumption from those cases. Today we simply acknowledge what has long been evident and was evident to the Ninth and Fifth Circuits and to the District Court.

The judgment of the Fifth Circuit is reversed.

Justice O'CONNOR, with whom Justice BREYER joins, concurring in the judgment.

Three Terms ago, we held in *Agostini v. Felton* that Title I, as applied in New York City, did not violate the Establishment Clause. I believe that *Agostini* likewise controls the constitutional inquiry respecting Title II presented here, and requires the reversal of the Court of Appeals' judgment that the program is unconstitutional as applied in Jefferson Parish, Louisiana. To the extent our decisions in *Meek v. Pittenger*, and *Wolman v. Walter*, are inconsistent with the Court's judgment today, I agree that those decisions should be overruled. I therefore concur in the judgment.

I write separately because, in my view, the plurality announces a rule of unprecedented breadth for the evaluation of Establishment Clause challenges to government school-aid programs. Reduced to its essentials, the plurality's rule states that government aid to religious schools does not have the effect of advancing religion so long as the aid is offered on a neutral basis and the aid is secular in content. The plurality also rejects the distinction between direct and indirect aid, and holds that the actual diversion of secular aid by a religious school to the advancement of its religious mission is permissible. Although the expansive scope of the plurality's rule is troubling, two specific aspects of the opinion compel me to write separately. First, the plurality's treatment of neutrality comes close to assigning that factor singular importance in the future adjudication of Establishment Clause challenges to government school-aid programs. Second, the plurality's approval of actual diversion of government aid to religious indoctrination is in tension with our precedents and, in any event, unnecessary to decide the instant case. . . .

Justice SOUTER provides a comprehensive review of our Establishment Clause cases on government aid to religious institutions that is useful for its explanation of the various ways in which we have used the term "neutrality" in our decisions. Even if we at one time used the term "neutrality" in a descriptive sense to refer to those aid programs characterized by the requisite equipoise between support of religion and antagonism to religion, Justice SOUTER's discussion convincingly demonstrates that the evolution in the meaning of the term in our jurisprudence is cause to hesitate before equating the neutrality of recent decisions with the neutrality of old. As I have previously explained, neutrality is important, but it is by no means the only "axiom in the history and precedent of the Establishment Clause." *Rosenberger v. Rector and Visitors of Univ. of Va.,* 515 U.S. 819 (1995) (concurring opinion). Thus, I agree with Justice SOUTER's conclusion that our "most recent use of 'neutrality' to refer to generality or even-handedness of distribution is relevant in judging whether a benefit scheme so characterized should be seen as aiding a sectarian school's religious mission, but this neutrality is not alone sufficient to qualify the aid as constitutional."

I also disagree with the plurality's conclusion that actual diversion of government aid to religious indoctrination is consistent with the Establishment Clause. Although "[o]ur cases have permitted some government funding of secular functions performed by sectarian organizations," our decisions "provide no precedent for the use of public funds to finance religious activities." *Rosenberger.* . . .

I would adhere to the rule that we have applied in the context of textbook lending programs: To establish a First Amendment violation, plaintiffs must prove that the aid in question actually is, or has been, used for religious purposes. See *Meek, Allen.* Just as we held in *Agostini* that our more recent cases had undermined the assumptions underlying *Ball* and *Aguilar,* I would now hold that *Agostini* and the cases on which it relied have undermined the assumptions underlying *Meek* and *Wolman.* To be sure, *Agostini* only addressed the specific presumption that public-school employees teaching on the premises of religious schools would inevitably inculcate religion. Nevertheless, I believe that our definitive rejection of that presumption also stood for—or at least strongly pointed to—the broader proposition that such presumptions of religious indoctrination are normally inappropriate when evaluating neutral school-aid programs under the Establishment Clause. . . .

Given the important similarities between the Chapter 2 program here and the Title I program at issue in *Agostini,* respondents' Establishment Clause challenge must fail. As in *Agostini,* the Chapter 2 aid is allocated on the basis of neutral, secular criteria; the aid must be supplementary and cannot supplant non-Federal funds; no Chapter 2 funds ever reach the coffers of religious schools; the aid must be secular; any evidence of actual diversion is *de minimis*; and the program includes adequate safeguards. Regardless of whether these factors are constitutional requirements, they are surely sufficient to find that the program at issue here does not have the impermissible effect of advancing religion. For the same reasons, "this carefully constrained program also cannot reasonably be viewed as an endorsement of religion." *Agostini.* Accordingly, I concur in the judgment.

Justice SOUTER, with whom Justice STEVENS and Justice GINSBURG join, dissenting.

The First Amendment's Establishment Clause prohibits Congress (and, by incorporation, the States) from making any law respecting an establishment of religion. It has been held to prohibit not only the institution of an official church, but any government act favoring religion, a particular religion, or for that matter irreligion. Thus it bars the use of public funds for religious aid.

The establishment prohibition of government religious funding serves more than one end. It is meant to guarantee the right of individual conscience against compulsion, to protect the integrity of religion against the corrosion of secular support, and to preserve the unity of political society against the implied exclusion of the less favored and the antagonism of controversy over public support for religious causes.

These objectives are always in some jeopardy since the substantive principle of no aid to religion is not the only limitation on government action toward religion. Because the First Amendment also bars any prohibition of individual free exercise of religion, and because religious organizations cannot be isolated from the basic government functions that create the civil environment, it is as much necessary as it is difficult to draw lines between forbidden aid and lawful benefit. For more than 50 years, this Court has been attempting to draw these lines. Owing to the variety of factual circumstances in which the lines must be drawn, not all of the points creating the boundary have enjoyed self-evidence.

So far as the line drawn has addressed government aid to education, a few fundamental generalizations are nonetheless possible. There may be no aid supporting a sectarian school's religious exercise or the discharge of its religious mission, while aid of a secular character with no discernible benefit to such a sectarian objective is allowable. Because the religious and secular spheres largely overlap in the life of many such schools, the Court has tried to identify some facts likely to reveal the relative religious or secular intent or effect of the government benefits in particular circumstances. We have asked whether the government is acting neutrally in distributing its money, and about the form of the aid itself, its path from government to religious institution, its divertibility to religious nurture, its potential for reducing traditional expenditures of religious institutions, and its relative importance to the recipient, among other things.

In all the years of its effort, the Court has isolated no single test of constitutional sufficiency, and the question in every case addresses the substantive principle of no aid: what reasons are there to characterize this benefit as aid to the sectarian school in discharging its religious mission? Particular factual circumstances control, and the answer is a matter of judgment.

In what follows I will flesh out this summary, for this case comes at a time when our judgment requires perspective on how the Establishment Clause has come to be understood and applied. It is not just that a majority today mistakes the significance of facts that have led to conclusions of unconstitutionality in earlier cases, though I believe the Court commits error in failing to recognize the divertibility of funds to the service of religious objectives. What is more important is the view revealed in the plurality opinion, which espouses a new conception of neutrality as a practically sufficient test of constitutionality that would, if adopted by the Court, eliminate enquiry into a law's effects. The plurality position breaks fundamentally with Establishment Clause principle, and with the methodology painstakingly worked out in support of it. I mean to revisit that principle and describe the methodology at some length, lest there be any question about the rupture that the plurality view would cause. From that new view of the law, and from a majority's mistaken application of the old, I respectfully dissent. . . .

[I]n the Court's classic summation delivered in *Everson v. Board of Education*, [330 U.S. 1 (1947)], its first opinion directly addressing standards governing aid to religious schools: "The 'establishment of religion' clause of the First

Amendment means at least this: Neither a state nor the Federal Government can set up a church. Neither can pass laws which aid one religion, aid all religions, or prefer one religion over another. Neither can force nor influence a person to go to or to remain away from church against his will or force him to profess a belief or disbelief in any religion. No person can be punished for entertaining or professing religious beliefs or disbeliefs, for church attendance or non-attendance. No tax in any amount, large or small, can be levied to support any religious activities or institutions, whatever they may be called, or whatever form they may adopt to teach or practice religion. Neither a state nor the Federal Government can, openly or secretly, participate in the affairs of any religious organizations or groups and vice versa. In the words of Jefferson, the clause against establishment of religion by law was intended to erect 'a wall of separation between Church and State.' " The most directly pertinent doctrinal statements here are these: no government "can pass laws which aid one religion [or] all religions. No tax in any amount can be levied to support any religious activities or institutions whatever form they may adopt to teach religion." Thus, the principle of "no aid," with which no one in *Everson* disagreed. . . .

After *Everson* and *Allen*, the state of the law applying the Establishment Clause to public expenditures producing some benefit to religious schools was this:

1. Government aid to religion is forbidden, and tax revenue may not be used to support a religious school or religious teaching.

2. Government provision of such paradigms of universally general welfare benefits as police and fire protection does not count as aid to religion.

3. Whether a law's benefit is sufficiently close to universally general welfare paradigms to be classified with them, as distinct from religious aid, is a function of the purpose and effect of the challenged law in all its particularity. The judgment is not reducible to the application of any formula. Evenhandedness of distribution as between religious and secular beneficiaries is a relevant factor, but not a sufficiency test of constitutionality. There is no rule of religious equal protection to the effect that any expenditure for the benefit of religious school students is necessarily constitutional so long as public school pupils are favored on ostensibly identical terms.

4. Government must maintain neutrality as to religion, "neutrality" being a conclusory label for the required position of government as neither aiding religion nor impeding religious exercise by believers. "Neutrality" was not the name of any test to identify permissible action, and in particular, was not synonymous with evenhandedness in conferring benefit on the secular as well as the religious.

Today, the substantive principle of no aid to religious mission remains the governing understanding of the Establishment Clause as applied to public benefits inuring to religious schools. The governing opinions on the subject in the 35 years since *Allen* have never challenged this principle. The cases have, however, recognized that in actual Establishment Clause litigation over school aid legislation, there is no pure aid to religion and no purely secular welfare benefit; the effects of the laws fall somewhere in between, with the judicial task being to make a realistic allocation between the two possibilities. The Court's decisions demonstrate its repeated attempts to isolate considerations relevant in classifying particular benefits as between those that do not discernibly support or threaten support of a school's religious mission, and those that cross or threaten to cross the line into support for religion.

The most deceptively familiar of those considerations is "neutrality," the presence or absence of which, in some sense, we have addressed from the moment of *Everson* itself. I say "some sense," for we have used the term in at least three ways in our cases, and an understanding of the term's evolution will help to explain the concept as it is understood today, as well as the limits of its significance in Establishment Clause analysis. "Neutrality" has been employed as a term to describe the requisite state of government equipoise between the forbidden encouragement and discouragement of religion; to characterize a benefit or aid as secular; and to indicate evenhandedness in distributing it. . . .

In sum, "neutrality" originally entered this field of jurisprudence as a conclusory term, a label for the required relationship between the government and religion as a state of equipoise between government as ally and government as adversary. Reexamining *Everson*'s paradigm cases to derive a prescriptive guideline, we first determined that "neutral" aid was secular, nonideological, or unrelated to religious education. Our subsequent reexamination of *Everson* and *Allen*, beginning in [*Committee for Public Education and Religious Freedom v.*] *Nyquest*, [413 U.S. 756 (1973),] and culminating in *Mueller* and most recently in *Agostini*, recast neutrality as a concept of "evenhandedness."

There is, of course, good reason for considering the generality of aid and the evenhandedness of its distribution in making close calls between benefits that in purpose or effect support a school's religious mission and those that do not. This is just what *Everson* did. Even when the disputed practice falls short of *Everson*'s paradigms, the breadth of evenhanded distribution is one pointer toward the law's purpose, since on the face of it aid distributed generally and without a religious criterion is less likely to be meant to aid religion than a benefit going only to religious institutions or people. And, depending on the breadth of distribution, looking to evenhandedness is a way of asking whether a benefit can reasonably be seen to aid religion in fact; we do not regard the postal system as aiding religion, even though parochial schools get mail. Given the legitimacy of considering evenhandedness, then, there is no reason to avoid the term "neutrality" to refer to it. But one crucial point must be borne in mind.

In the days when "neutral" was used in *Everson*'s sense of equipoise, neutrality was tantamount to constitutionality; the term was conclusory, but when it applied it meant that the government's position was constitutional under the Establishment Clause. This is not so at all, however, under the most recent use of "neutrality" to refer to generality or evenhandedness of distribution. This kind of neutrality is relevant in judging whether a benefit scheme so characterized should be seen as aiding a sectarian school's religious mission, but this neutrality is not alone sufficient to qualify the aid as constitutional. It is to be considered only along with other characteristics of aid, its administration, its recipients, or its potential that have been emphasized over the years as indicators of just how religious the intent and effect of a given aid scheme really is. Thus, the basic principle of establishment scrutiny of aid remains the principle as stated in *Everson*, that there may be no public aid to religion or support for the religious mission of any institution. . . .

[Our] doctrinal history leaves one point clear beyond peradventure: together with James Madison we have consistently understood the Establishment Clause to impose a substantive prohibition against public aid to religion and, hence, to the religious mission of sectarian schools. Evenhandedness neutrality is one, nondispositive pointer toward an intent and (to a lesser degree) probable effect on the permissible side of the line between forbidden aid and general public welfare benefit. Other pointers are facts about the religious mission and education level of benefited schools and their pupils, the pathway by which a benefit travels from public treasury to educational effect, the form and content of the aid, its adaptability to religious ends, and its effects on school budgets. The object of all enquiries into such matters is the same whatever the particular circumstances: is the benefit intended to aid in providing the religious element of the education and is it likely to do so?

The substance of the law has thus not changed since *Everson*. Emphasis on one sort of fact or another has varied depending on the perceived utility of the enquiry, but all that has been added is repeated explanation of relevant considerations, confirming that our predecessors were right in their prophecies that no simple test would emerge to allow easy application of the establishment principle.

The plurality, however, would reject that lesson. The majority misapplies it.

The nub of the plurality's new position is this: "[I]f the government, seeking to further some legitimate secular purpose, offers aid on the same terms, without regard to religion, to all who adequately further that purpose, then it is fair to say that any aid going to a religious recipient only has the effect of furthering that secular purpose. The government, in crafting such an aid program, has had to conclude that a given level of aid is necessary to further that purpose among secular recipients and has provided no more than that same level to religious recipients." As a break with consistent doctrine the plurality's new criterion is unequaled in the history of Establishment Clause interpretation. Simple on its face, it appears to take evenhandedness neutrality and in practical terms promote it to a single and sufficient test for the establishment constitutionality of school aid. Even on its own terms, its errors are manifold, and attention to at least three of its mistaken assumptions will show the degree to which the plurality's proposal would replace the principle of no aid with a formula for generous religious support.

First, the plurality treats an external observer's attribution of religious support to the government as the sole impermissible effect of a government aid scheme. While perceived state endorsement of religion is undoubtedly a relevant concern under the Establishment Clause, it is certainly not the only one. *Everson* made this clear from the start: secret aid to religion by the government is also barred. State aid not attributed to the government would still violate a taxpayer's liberty of conscience, threaten to corrupt religion, and generate disputes over aid. . . .

Second, the plurality apparently assumes as a fact that equal amounts of aid to religious and nonreligious schools will have exclusively secular and equal effects, on both external perception and on incentives to attend different schools. But there is no reason to believe that this will be the case; the effects of same-terms aid may not be confined to the secular sphere at all. This is the reason that we have long recognized that unrestricted aid to religious schools will support religious teaching in addition to secular education, a fact that would be true no matter what the supposedly secular purpose of the law might be.

Third, the plurality assumes that per capita distribution rules safeguard the same principles as independent, private choices. But that is clearly not so. We approved university scholarships in *Witters* because we found them close to giving a government employee a paycheck and allowing him to spend it as he chose, but a per capita aid program is a far cry from awarding scholarships to individuals, one of whom makes an independent private choice. Not the least of the significant differences between per capita aid and aid individually determined and directed is the right and genuine opportunity of the recipient to choose not to give the aid. To hold otherwise would be to license the government to donate funds to churches based on the number of their members, on the patent fiction of independent private choice.

The plurality's mistaken assumptions explain and underscore its sharp break with the Framers' understanding of establishment and this Court's consistent interpretative course. Under the plurality's regime, little would be left of the right of conscience against compelled support for religion; the more massive the aid the more potent would be the influence of the government on the teaching mission; the more generous the support, the more divisive would be the resentments of those resisting religious support, and those religions without school systems ready to claim their fair share.

The plurality's conception of evenhandedness does not, however, control the case, whose disposition turns on the misapplication of accepted categories of school aid analysis. The facts most obviously relevant to the Chapter 2 scheme in Jefferson Parish are those showing divertibility and actual diversion in the circumstance of pervasively sectarian religious schools. The type of aid, the structure of the program, and the lack of effective safeguards clearly demonstrate the divertibility of the aid. While little is known about its use, owing to the anemic enforcement system in the parish, even the thin record before us reveals that actual diversion occurred. . . .

The plurality would break with the law. The majority misapplies it. That misapplication is, however, the only consolation in the case, which reaches an erroneous result but does not stage a doctrinal coup. But there is no mistaking the abandonment of doctrine that would occur if the plurality were to become a majority. It is beyond question that the plurality's notion of evenhandedness neutrality as a practical guarantee of the validity of aid to sectarian schools would be the end of the principle of no aid to the schools' religious mission. And if that were not so obvious it would become so after reflecting on the plurality's thoughts about diversion and about giving attention to the pervasiveness of a school's sectarian teaching.

The plurality is candid in pointing out the extent of actual diversion of Chapter 2 aid to religious use in the case before us, and equally candid in saying it does not matter. To the plurality there is nothing wrong with aiding a school's religious mission; the only question is whether religious teaching obtains its tax support under a formally evenhanded criterion of distribution. The principle of no aid to religious teaching has no independent significance.

And if this were not enough to prove that no aid in religious school aid is dead under the plurality's First Amendment, the point is nailed down in the plurality's attack on the legitimacy of considering a school's pervasively sectarian character when judging whether aid to the school is likely to aid its religious mission. The relevance of this consideration is simply a matter of common sense: where religious indoctrination pervades school activities of children and adolescents, it takes great care to be able to aid the school without supporting the doctrinal effort. This is obvious. The plurality nonetheless condemns any enquiry into the pervasiveness of doctrinal content as a remnant of anti-Catholic bigotry (as if evangelical Protestant schools and Orthodox Jewish yeshivas were never pervasively sectarian), and it equates a refusal to aid religious schools with hostility to religion (as if aid to religious teaching were not opposed in this very case by at least one religious respondent and numerous religious amici curiae in a tradition claiming descent from Roger Williams). My concern with these arguments goes not so much to their details as it does to the fact that the plurality's choice to employ imputations of bigotry and irreligion as terms in the Court's debate makes one point clear: that in rejecting the principle of no aid to a school's religious mission the plurality is attacking the most fundamental assumption underlying the Establishment Clause, that government can in fact operate with neutrality in its relation to religion. I believe that it can, and so respectfully dissent.

# 7

## THE FOURTH AMENDMENT GUARANTEE AGAINST UNREASONABLE SEARCHES AND SEIZURES

### A. REQUIREMENTS FOR A WARRANT AND REASONABLE SEARCHES AND SEIZURES

In *Wilson v. Layne* (1999) (excerpted below) the Court held that police violate individuals' constitutionally protected privacy interests under the Fourth Amendment when they invite members of the media to film and photograph their execution of arrest warrants in private homes. However, writing for the Court, Chief Justice Rehnquist held that at the time this case originated—in the early 1990s—the law was unclear, and therefore police enjoyed qualified immunity from suits for damages; henceforth, though, police are liable for allowing the media to accompany them when executing arrest and search warrants in private homes. In a related decision, *Hanlon v. Berger*, 119 S.Ct. 1692 (1999), the Court unanimously ruled in a *per curiam* opinion that federal agents had violated the Fourth Amendment's guarantees for personal privacy by allowing CNN to film the search of a ranch for evidence of the illegal possession of wildlife. But, under *Wilson*, the Court also held that here the agents enjoyed qualified immunity from suits for damages.

In its 2000–2001 term the Court will consider, in *Illinois v. Mcarthur* (No. 99-1132), whether police, while waiting for a search warrant, may secure a dwelling and not allow the resident to enter unaccompanied, without violating the Fourth Amendment. Mcarthur's estranged wife told the police that there were drugs in a trailer home from which she was removing her belongings under their protection. Mcarthur, however, refused to allow the police to search the trailer without a warrant. His trailer was subsequently searched and he was arrested for drug possession. A state court, however, concluded that the police action was unreasonable because Mcarthur was not in custody and the police violated his freedom of movement and possessory interests in the trailer.

## *Wilson v. Layne*
### 119 S.Ct. 1692 (1999)

In early 1992, the attorney general of the United States approved "Operation Gunsmoke," a national fugitive apprehension program in which U.S. marshals worked with state and local police, as well as the media, to apprehend dangerous criminals. One of the dangerous fugitives identified as a target of "Operation Gunsmoke" was Dominic Wilson, the son of petitioners Charles and Geraldine Wilson. Dominic Wilson had violated his probation on previous felony charges, and the police computer listed "caution indicators that he was likely to be armed, to resist arrest, and to assaul[t] police." The computer also listed his address as 909 North StoneStreet Avenue in Rockville, Maryland. Unknown to the police, however, this was actually the home of his parents. In April 1992 a state court issued three arrest warrants for Dominic Wilson. Subsequently, in the early morning hours of April 16, 1992, a Gunsmoke team, along with a reporter and a photographer from the *Washington Post* who had been invited to accompany them, drove to Wilson's alleged address. At 6:45 A.M., the officers, with media representatives in tow, entered the dwelling at 909 North StoneStreet Avenue, where the petitioners were still in bed when they heard the officers enter. Charles Wilson, dressed only in a pair of briefs, ran into the living room to investigate and discovered at least five men in street clothes with guns in his living room. He angrily demanded that they state their business and repeatedly cursed the officers. Believing him to be an angry Dominic Wilson, the officers quickly subdued him on the floor. Once their protective sweep was completed, the officers learned that Dominic Wilson was not in the house and they departed. But, during the time that the officers were in the home, the *Washington Post* photographer took numerous pictures, including of the confrontation between the police and Charles Wilson; however, none were published. Wilson later sued the police for money damages under *Bivens v. Six Unknown Fed. Narcotics Agents*, 403 U.S. 388 (1971), and Section 1983 of the U.S. Code, which authorizes suits for damages when officials violate individuals' constitutional rights. Attorneys for the police countered that the officers enjoyed qualified immunity because they had not knowingly violated any constitutional rights by allowing members of the media to accompany them. A district court rejected the latter argument but an appellate court reversed. Wilson appealed to the Supreme Court, which granted review and affirmed the appellate court's ruling.

The Court's decision was eight to one, and its opinion was delivered by Chief Justice Rehnquist. Justice Stevens issued a separate opinion in part concurring and dissenting.

Chief Justice REHNQUIST delivered the opinion of the Court.

While executing an arrest warrant in a private home, police officers invited representatives of the media to accompany them. We hold that such a "media ride along" does violate the Fourth Amendment, but that because the state of the law was not clearly established at the time the search in this case took place, the officers are entitled to the defense of qualified immunity. . . .

The petitioners sued the federal officials under *Bivens* and the state officials under Section 1983. Both *Bivens* and Section 1983 allow a plaintiff to seek money damages from government officials who have violated his Fourth Amendment rights. But government officials performing discretionary functions generally are granted a qualified immunity and are "shielded from liability for civil damages insofar as their conduct does not violate clearly established statutory or constitutional rights of which a reasonable person would have known." *Harlow v. Fitzgerald*, 457 U.S. 800 (1982).

Although this case involves suits under both Section 1983 and *Bivens*, the qualified immunity analysis is identical under either cause of action. A court evaluating a claim of qualified immunity "must first determine whether the plaintiff has alleged the deprivation of an actual constitutional right at all, and if so, proceed to determine whether that right was clearly established at the time of the alleged violation." *Conn. v. Gabbert*, [119 S.Ct. 1292] (1999). . . .

The Fourth Amendment embodies [a] centuries-old principle of respect for the privacy of the home: "The right of the people to be secure in their persons, houses, papers, and effects, against unreasonable searches and seizures, shall not be violated, and no Warrants shall issue, but upon probable cause, supported by Oath or affirmation, and particularly describing the place to be searched, and the persons or things to be seized."

Our decisions have applied these basic principles of the Fourth Amendment to situations, like those in this case, in which police enter a home under the authority of an arrest warrant in order to take into custody the suspect named in the warrant. In *Payton v. New York*, 445 U.S. 573 (1980), we noted that although clear in its protection of the home, the common-law tradition at the time of the drafting of the Fourth Amendment was ambivalent on the question of whether police could enter a home without a warrant. We were ultimately persuaded that the "overriding respect for the sanctity of the home that has been embedded in our traditions since the origins of the Republic" meant that absent a warrant or exigent circumstances, police could not enter a home to make an arrest. We decided that "an arrest warrant founded on probable cause implicitly carries with it the limited authority to enter a dwelling in which the suspect lives when there is reason to believe the suspect is within."

Here, of course, the officers had such a warrant, and they were undoubtedly entitled to enter the Wilson home in order to execute the arrest warrant for Dominic Wilson. But it does not necessarily follow that they were entitled to bring a newspaper reporter and a photographer with them. . . .

Respondents argue that the presence of the *Washington Post* reporters in the Wilsons' home nonetheless served a number of legitimate law enforcement purposes. They first assert that officers should be able to exercise reasonable discretion about when it would "further their law enforcement mission to permit members of the news media to accompany them in executing a warrant." But this claim ignores the importance of the right of residential privacy at the core of the Fourth Amendment. It may well be that media ride-alongs further the law enforcement objectives of the police in a general sense, but that is not the same as furthering the purposes of the search. Were such generalized "law enforcement objectives" themselves sufficient to trump the Fourth Amendment, the protections guaranteed by that Amendment's text would be significantly watered down.

Respondents next argue that the presence of third parties could serve the law enforcement purpose of publicizing the government's efforts to combat crime, and facilitate accurate reporting on law enforcement activities. There is certainly language in our opinions interpreting the First Amendment which points to the importance of "the press" in informing the general public about the administration of criminal justice. . . . But the Fourth Amendment also protects a very important right, and in the present case it is in terms of that right that the media ride-alongs must be judged.

Finally, respondents argue that the presence of third parties could serve in some situations to minimize police abuses and protect suspects, and also to protect the safety of the officers. While it might be reasonable for police officers to themselves videotape home entries as part of a "quality control" effort to ensure that the rights of homeowners are being respected, or even to preserve evidence, such a situation is significantly different from the media presence in this case. The *Washington Post* reporters in the Wilsons' home were working on a story for their own purposes. They were not present for the purpose of protecting the officers, much less the Wilsons. A private photographer was acting for private purposes, as evidenced in part by the fact that the newspaper and not the police retained the photographs. Thus, although the presence of third parties during the execution of a warrant may in some circumstances be constitutionally permissible, the presence of these third parties was not. . . .

Since the police action in this case violated the petitioners' Fourth Amendment right, we now must decide whether this right was clearly established at the time of the search. As noted above, government officials performing discretionary functions generally are granted a qualified immunity and are "shielded from liability for civil damages insofar as their conduct does not violate clearly established statutory or constitutional rights of which a reasonable person would have known." *Harlow v. Fitzgerald.* What this means in practice is that "whether an official protected by qualified immunity may be held personally liable for an allegedly unlawful official action generally turns on the 'objective legal reasonableness' of the action, assessed in light of the legal rules that were 'clearly established' at the time it was taken." *Anderson v. Creighton,* 483 U.S. 635 (1987).

In *Anderson,* we explained that what "clearly established" means in this context depends largely "upon the level of generality at which the relevant 'legal rule' is to be established." . . .

We hold that it was not unreasonable for a police officer in April 1992 to have believed that bringing media observers along during the execution of an arrest warrant (even in a home) was lawful. First, the constitutional question presented by this case is by no means open and shut. . . .

Second, although media ride-alongs of one sort or another had apparently become a common police practice, in 1992 there were no judicial opinions holding that this practice became unlawful when it entered a home. . . .

Finally, important to our conclusion was the reliance by the United States marshals in this case on a Marshal's Service ride-along policy which explicitly contemplated that media who engaged in ride-alongs might enter private homes with their cameras as part of fugitive apprehension arrests. . . . Such a policy, of course, could not make reasonable a belief that was contrary to a decided body of case law. But here the state of the law as to third parties accompanying police on home entries was at best undeveloped, and it was not unreasonable for law enforcement officers to look and rely on their formal ride-along policies. . . .

For the foregoing reasons, the judgment of the Court of Appeals is affirmed.


Justice STEVENS, concurring in part and dissenting in part.

In my view, . . . the homeowner's right to protection against this type of tres-pass was clearly established long before April 16, 1992. My sincere respect for the competence of the typical member of the law enforcement profession pre-cludes my assent to the suggestion that "a reasonable officer could have believed that bringing members of the media into a home during the execution of an arrest warrant was lawful." I therefore disagree with the Court's resolution of the con-flict in the Circuits on the qualified immunity issue. The clarity of the constitu-tional rule, a federal statute, common-law decisions, and the testimony of the senior law enforcement officer all support my position that it has long been clearly established that officers may not bring third parties into private homes to witness the execution of a warrant. . . .

I respectfully dissent.


# B. EXCEPTIONS TO THE WARRANT REQUIREMENT

In a brief *per curiam* opinion in *Maryland v. Dyson*, 119 S.Ct. 2013 (1999), the Court underscored that the automobile exception to the Fourth Amendment's warrant requirement does not require police to obtain a war-rant to search a car when they have probable cause to believe that it con-tains contraband. In doing so, the Court reversed a state court ruling that, unless exigent circumstances justify a warrantless search, police must obtain a warrant before conducting a search, even though they have prob-able cause to believe that the automobile contains contraband. As in *Penn-sylvania v. Labron*, 518 U.S. 938 (1996), the Court repeated that "the automobile exception does not have a separate exigency requirement: 'If a car is readily mobile and probable cause exists to believe it contains contra-band, the Fourth Amendment permits police to search the vehicle without more.'" Justice Breyer dissented and would have granted oral arguments in the case.

In another brief *per curiam* opinion, in *Flippo v. West Virginia*, 120 S.Ct. 7 (1999), the Court unanimously overturned a state court decision that upheld warrantless police searches of murder crime scenes. In rejecting that court's "murder crime scene" exception for warrantless searches, the Court reaffirmed the holding in *Mincey v. Arizona*, 437 U.S. 385 (1978).

In another unanimous decision, the Court refused to extend the scope of permissible stopping and frisking of individuals by police, as set forth in *Terry v. Ohio*, 392 U.S. 1 (1968), and *Adams v. Williams*, 407 U.S. 590 (1972). *Adams* had extended *Terry*'s exception to the Fourth Amendment in upholding the stopping and frisking of an individual by an officer based on a tip from a known informant that he was carrying a gun. However, in *Florida v. J.L.*, 120 S.Ct. 1375 (2000), the Court held unconstitutional the stopping and frisking of an individual for a gun based on a police officer's receiving an anonymous tip that a young black male wearing a plaid shirt at a bus stop was carrying a gun. Writing for the Court, Justice Ginsburg ruled that anonymous tips, unless accompanied by other specific indicators of reliability, fall short of providing a basis for reasonable suspicion to justify officers' stopping and frisking of individuals.

In its 1999–2000 term the Court also considered, in *Illinois v. Wardlow* (excerpted below), whether an individual's flight from police justifies their stopping the individual under the important stop-and-frisk ruling in *Terry v. Ohio*, 392 U.S. 1 (1968) (excerpted in Vol. 2, Ch. 7). In *Bond v. United States* (excerpted below) the Court also drew the line on suspicionless searches by police of luggage on public transportation in an opinion by Chief Justice Rehnquist; Justices Breyer and Scalia dissented.

## *Illinois v. Wardlow*
### 120 S.Ct. 673 (2000)

Around noon in an area of Chicago known for drug trafficking, two uniformed police officers were riding in the last of a four-car police caravan when they noticed William Wardlow holding an opaque bag. After looking in their direction, Wardlow fled down an alley and the officers followed, eventually cornering him. During a pat-down search for weapons, one of the officers squeezed the bag and felt a heavy object, which turned out to be a .38-caliber handgun. At his trial, Wardlow's attorney moved to suppress the use of the gun as evidence on the ground that the officer did not have a "reasonable suspicion" to justify the search and seizure under *Terry v. Ohio*, 392 U.S. 1 (1968). The trial court disagreed, but a state appellate court reversed Wardlow's conviction and the Illinois Supreme Court affirmed, concluding that a sudden flight from police, even in a high crime area, does not create a "reasonable suspicion" to justify a *Terry* stop. The state appealed and the Supreme Court granted review.

The state supreme court's decision was reversed in a five to four decision, with the opinion delivered by Chief Justice Rehnquist. Justice Stevens filed an opinion in part concurring and dissenting, which Justices Breyer, Ginsburg, and Souter joined.

Chief Justice REHNQUIST delivered the opinion of the Court.

This case, involving a brief encounter between a citizen and a police officer on a public street, is governed by the analysis we first applied in *Terry* [*v. Ohio*]. In *Terry*, we held that an officer may, consistent with the Fourth Amendment, conduct a brief, investigatory stop when the officer has a reasonable, articulable suspicion that criminal activity is afoot. While "reasonable suspicion" is a less demanding standard than probable cause and requires a showing considerably less than preponderance of the evidence, the Fourth Amendment requires at least a minimal level of objective justification for making the stop.

An individual's presence in an area of expected criminal activity, standing alone, is not enough to support a reasonable, particularized suspicion that the person is committing a crime. But officers are not required to ignore the relevant characteristics of a location in determining whether the circumstances are sufficiently suspicious to warrant further investigation. . . .

In this case, moreover, it was not merely respondent's presence in an area of heavy narcotics trafficking that aroused the officers' suspicion but his unprovoked flight upon noticing the police. Our cases have also recognized that nervous, evasive behavior is a pertinent factor in determining reasonable suspicion. Headlong flight—wherever it occurs—is the consummate act of evasion: it is not necessarily indicative of wrongdoing, but it is certainly suggestive of such. In reviewing the propriety of an officer's conduct, courts do not have available empirical studies dealing with inferences drawn from suspicious behavior, and we cannot reasonably demand scientific certainty from judges or law enforcement officers where none exists. Thus, the determination of reasonable suspicion must be based on commonsense judgments and inferences about human behavior. We conclude Officer Nolan was justified in suspecting that Wardlow was involved in criminal activity, and, therefore, in investigating further. . . .

Justice STEVENS, with whom Justice SOUTER, Justice GINSBURG, and Justice BREYER join, concurring in part and dissenting in part.

Guided by that totality-of-the-circumstances test, the Court concludes that Officer Nolan had reasonable suspicion to stop respondent. In this respect, my view differs from the Court's. The entire justification for the stop is articulated in the brief testimony of Officer Nolan. Some facts are perfectly clear; others are not. This factual insufficiency leads me to conclude that the Court's judgment is mistaken.

Nolan was part of an eight-officer, four-car caravan patrol team. The officers were headed for "one of the areas in the 11th District [of Chicago] that's high [in] narcotics traffic." The reason why four cars were in the caravan was that "[n]ormally in these different areas there's an enormous amount of people, sometimes lookouts, customers." Officer Nolan testified that he was in uniform on that day, but he did not recall whether he was driving a marked or an unmarked car.

Officer Nolan and his partner were in the last of the four patrol cars that "were all caravaning eastbound down Van Buren." Nolan first observed respondent "in front of 4035 West Van Buren." Wardlow "looked in our direction and began fleeing." Nolan then "began driving southbound down the street observing [respondent] running through the gangway and the alley southbound," and observed that Wardlow was carrying a white, opaque bag under his arm. After the car turned south and intercepted respondent as he "ran right towards us," Officer Nolan stopped him and conducted a "protective search," which revealed that the bag under respondent's arm contained a loaded handgun.

This terse testimony is most noticeable for what it fails to reveal. Though asked whether he was in a marked or unmarked car, Officer Nolan could not recall the answer. He was not asked whether any of the other three cars in the caravan were marked, or whether any of the other seven officers were in uniform. Though he explained that the size of the caravan was because "[n]ormally in these different areas there's an enormous amount of people, sometimes lookouts, customers," Officer Nolan did not testify as to whether anyone besides Wardlow was nearby 4035 West Van Buren. Nor is it clear that that address was the intended destination of the caravan. As the Appellate Court of Illinois interpreted the record, "it appears that the officers were simply driving by, on their way to some unidentified location, when they noticed defendant standing at 4035 West Van Buren." Officer Nolan's testimony also does not reveal how fast the officers were driving. It does not indicate whether he saw respondent notice the other patrol cars. And it does not say whether the caravan, or any part of it, had already passed Wardlow by before he began to run. . . .

No other factors sufficiently support a finding of reasonable suspicion. . . . Officer Nolan did testify that he expected to find "an enormous amount of people," including drug customers or lookouts, and the Court points out that "[i]t was in this context that Officer Nolan decided to investigate Wardlow after observing him flee." This observation, in my view, lends insufficient weight to the reasonable suspicion analysis; indeed, in light of the absence of testimony that anyone else was nearby when respondent began to run, this observation points in the opposite direction. . . .

It is the State's burden to articulate facts sufficient to support reasonable suspicion. In my judgment, Illinois has failed to discharge that burden. I am not persuaded that the mere fact that someone standing on a sidewalk looked in the direction of a passing car before starting to run is sufficient to justify a forcible stop and frisk.

# Bond v. United States
## 120 S.Ct. 1462 (2000)

The facts are stated by Chief Justice Rehnquist in the opinion of the Court, reversing the appellate court's decision. Justice Breyer filed a dissenting opinion, which Justice Scalia joined.

Chief Justice REHNQUIST delivered the opinion of the Court.

Petitioner Steven Dewayne Bond was a passenger on a Greyhound bus that left California bound for Little Rock, Arkansas. The bus stopped, as it was required to do, at the permanent Border Patrol checkpoint in Sierra Blanca, Texas. Border Patrol Agent Cesar Cantu boarded the bus to check the immigration status of its passengers. After reaching the back of the bus, having satisfied himself that the passengers were lawfully in the United States, Agent Cantu began walking toward the front. Along the way, he squeezed the soft luggage which passengers had placed in the overhead storage space above the seats.

As Agent Cantu inspected the luggage in the compartment above petitioner's seat, he squeezed a green canvas bag and noticed that it contained a "brick-like" object. Petitioner admitted that the bag was his and agreed to allow Agent Cantu to open it. Upon opening the bag, Agent Cantu discovered a "brick" of methamphetamine. The brick had been wrapped in duct tape until it was oval-shaped and then rolled in a pair of pants.

Petitioner was indicted for conspiracy to possess, and possession with intent to distribute, methamphetamine. He moved to suppress the drugs, arguing that Agent Cantu conducted an illegal search of his bag. Petitioner's motion was denied, and the District Court found him guilty on both counts and sentenced him to 57 months in prison. On appeal, he conceded that other passengers had access to his bag, but contended that Agent Cantu manipulated the bag in a way that other passengers would not. The Court of Appeals rejected this argument. . . . We granted *certiorari*, and now reverse.

[T]he Government asserts that by exposing his bag to the public, petitioner lost a reasonable expectation that his bag would not be physically manipulated. The Government relies on our decisions in *California v. Ciraolo*, [476 U.S. 207 (1986)], and *Florida v. Riley*, 488 U.S. 445 (1989), for the proposition that matters open to public observation are not protected by the Fourth Amendment. In *Ciraolo*, we held that police observation of a backyard from a plane flying at an altitude of 1,000 feet did not violate a reasonable expectation of privacy. Similarly, in *Riley*, we relied on *Ciraolo* to hold that police observation of a greenhouse in a home's curtilage from a helicopter passing at an altitude of 400 feet did not violate the Fourth Amendment. We reasoned that the property was "not necessarily protected from inspection that involves no physical invasion," and determined that because any member of the public could have lawfully observed the defendants' property by flying overhead, the defendants' expectation of privacy was "not reasonable and not one 'that society is prepared to honor.' "

But *Ciraolo* and *Riley* are different from this case because they involved only visual, as opposed to tactile, observation. Physically invasive inspection is simply more intrusive than purely visual inspection. For example, in *Terry v. Ohio*, 392 U.S. 1 (1968), we stated that a "careful [tactile] exploration of the outer surfaces of a person's clothing all over his or her body" is a "serious intrusion upon the sanctity of the person, which may inflict great indignity and arouse strong resentment, and is not to be undertaken lightly." Although Agent Cantu did not "frisk" petitioner's person, he did conduct a probing tactile examination of petitioner's carry-on luggage. Obviously, petitioner's bag was not part of his person. But travelers are particularly concerned about their carry-on luggage; they generally use it to transport personal items that, for whatever reason, they prefer to keep close at hand. . . .

Our Fourth Amendment analysis embraces two questions. First, we ask whether the individual, by his conduct, has exhibited an actual expectation of privacy; that is, whether he has shown that "he [sought] to preserve [something] as private." Here, petitioner sought to preserve privacy by using an opaque bag and placing that bag directly above his seat. Second, we inquire whether the individual's expectation of privacy is "one that society is prepared to recognize as reasonable." When a bus passenger places a bag in an overhead bin, he expects that other passengers or bus employees may move it for one reason or another. Thus, a bus passenger clearly expects that his bag may be handled. He does not expect that other passengers or bus employees will, as a matter of course, feel the bag in an exploratory manner. But this is exactly what the agent did here. We therefore hold that the agent's physical manipulation of petitioner's bag violated the Fourth Amendment.

Justice BREYER, with whom Justice SCALIA joins, dissenting.

Does a traveler who places a soft-sided bag in the shared overhead storage compartment of a bus have a "reasonable expectation" that strangers will not push, pull, prod, squeeze, or otherwise manipulate his luggage? Unlike the majority, I believe that he does not. . . .

[A]n individual cannot reasonably expect privacy in respect to objects or activities that he "knowingly exposes to the public." Indeed, the Court has said that it is not objectively reasonable to expect privacy if "[a]ny member of the public could have" used his senses to detect "everything that th[e] officers observed." *California v. Ciraolo.* Thus, it has held that the fact that strangers may look down at fenced-in property from an aircraft or sift through garbage bags on a public street can justify a similar police intrusion. Consider, too, the accepted police practice of using dogs to sniff for drugs hidden inside luggage. . . .

Of course, the agent's purpose here—searching for drugs—differs dramatically from the intention of a driver or fellow passenger who squeezes a bag in the process of making more room for another parcel. But in determining whether an expectation of privacy is reasonable, it is the effect, not the purpose, that matters. . . .

If we are to depart from established legal principles, we should not begin here. At best, this decision will lead to a constitutional jurisprudence of "squeezes," thereby complicating further already complex Fourth Amendment law, increasing the difficulty of deciding ordinary criminal matters, and hindering the administrative guidance (with its potential for control of unreasonable police practices) that a less complicated jurisprudence might provide. . . .

# C. THE SPECIAL PROBLEMS OF AUTOMOBILES IN A MOBILE SOCIETY

In its 2000–2001 term the Court will consider the constitutionality of roadblocks for drugs and whether they constitute an unreasonable search and seizure in violation of the Fourth Amendment. The city of Indianapolis established roadblocks to catch drug dealers. During a roadblock, police peer through car windows and ask for drivers' licenses and registrations, while a drug-sniffing dog circles the car. More than 1,150 cars stopped resulted in 55 drug arrests, and another 49 arrests were made for other offenses. A federal appellate court, however, ruled that the practice was unconstitutional because stopping an automobile is a seizure within the meaning of the Fourth Amendment and the roadblocks fail to meet the "individualized suspicion of wrongdoing" requirement, under *Chandler v. Miller*, 520 U.S. 305 (1997). The city appealed that decision, in *City of Indianapolis v. Edmond* (No. 99-1030), and the Court granted review.

The Court will also consider the application of the Fourth Amendment to arrests made for routine traffic stops in *Atwater v. Lago Vista* (No. 99-1408). Ms. Gail Atwater was arrested, handcuffed, and briefly jailed by a Lago Vista, Texas, police officer who stopped her car because neither she nor her two children were using seat belts. After spending an hour in jail, Ms. Atwater appeared before a magistrate and paid a fifty-dollar fine.

In *Wyoming v. Houghton* (excerpted below) the Court held that police may without a warrant search the belongings of passengers in cars if they have probable cause for doing so. And in *Florida v. White* (excerpted below), the Court held that the Fourth Amendment does not require police to obtain a warrant before seizing an automobile from a public place when they have probable cause to believe that it is forfeitable contraband.

## *Wyoming v. Houghton*
### 119 S.Ct. 1297 (1999)

In the early morning hours of July 23, 1995, a highway patrol officer stopped a car for speeding and having a faulty brake light. After noticing a syringe in the driver's shirt pocket, the officer instructed the driver and passegers to get out of the car and proceeded to search the car. The officer found the purse of one of the passengers, Sandra Houghton, on the back seat of the car and discovered inside it drugs and another syringe. Ms. Houghton was charged with felony drug possession, and at her trial, she moved to suppress the introduction of the evidence against her. The trial court dismissed her motion and she was convicted, but on appeal the Wyoming State Supreme Court reversed on the ground that the officer did not have probable cause to search the passengers' possessions. The state appealed, and the Supreme Court overruled the state supreme court's decision.

The Court's decision was six to three, and its opinion was delivered by Justice Scalia. Justice Breyer filed a concurring opinion, and Justice Stevens issued a dissenting opinion, which was joined by Justices Ginsburg and Souter.

Justice SCALIA delivered the opinion of the Court.

The Fourth Amendment protects "[t]he right of the people to be secure in their persons, houses, papers, and effects, against unreasonable searches and seizures." In determining whether a particular governmental action violates this provision, we inquire first whether the action was regarded as an unlawful search or seizure under the common law when the Amendment was framed. Where that inquiry yields no answer, we must evaluate the search or seizure under traditional standards of reasonableness by assessing, on the one hand, the degree to which it intrudes upon an individual's privacy and, on the other, the degree to which it is needed for the promotion of legitimate governmental interests.

It is uncontested in the present case that the police had probable cause to believe there were illegal drugs in the car. *Carroll v. United States*, 267 U.S. 132 (1925), similarly involved the warrantless search of a car that law enforcement officials had probable cause to believe contained contraband—in that case, bootleg liquor. The Court concluded that the Framers would have regarded such a search as reasonable in light of legislation enacted by Congress from 1789 through 1799—as well as subsequent legislation from the Founding era and beyond—that empowered customs officials to search any ship or vessel without a warrant if they had probable cause to believe that it contained goods subject to a duty. See also *United States v. Ross*, 456 U.S. 798 (1982). Thus, the Court held that "contraband goods concealed and illegally transported in an automobile or other vehicle may be searched for without a warrant" where probable cause exists.

We have furthermore read the historical evidence to show that the Framers would have regarded as reasonable (if there was probable cause) the warrantless search of containers *within* an automobile. In *Ross*, we upheld as reasonable the warrantless search of a paper bag and leather pouch found in the trunk of the defendant's car by officers who had probable cause to believe that the trunk contained drugs. . . . *Ross* summarized its holding as follows: "If probable cause justifies the search of a lawfully stopped vehicle, it justifies the search of *every part of the vehicle and its contents* that may conceal the object of the search." And our later cases describing *Ross* have characterized it as applying broadly to *all* containers within a car, without qualification as to ownership. See, e.g., *California v. Acevedo*, 500 U.S. 565 (1991). . . .

We hold that police officers with probable cause to search a car may inspect passengers' belongings found in the car that are capable of concealing the object of the search. The judgment of the Wyoming Supreme Court is reversed.

Justice STEVENS, with whom Justice SOUTER and Justice GINSBURG join, dissenting.

In all of our prior cases applying the automobile exception to the Fourth Amendment's warrant requirement, either the defendant was the operator of the vehicle and in custody of the object of the search, or no question was raised as to the defendant's ownership or custody. . . . [T]he Court's rights-restrictive approach is not dictated by precedent. For example, in *United States v. Ross*, we were concerned with the interest of the driver in the integrity of "his automobile," and we categorically rejected the notion that the scope of a warrantless search of a vehicle might be "defined by the nature of the container in which the contraband is secreted." "Rather, it is defined by the object of the search and the places in which there is probable cause to believe that it may be found." We thus disapproved of a possible container-based distinction between a man's pocket and a woman's pocketbook. Ironically, while we concluded in *Ross* that "[p]robable cause to believe that a container placed in the trunk of a taxi contains contraband or evidence does not justify a search of the entire cab," the rule the Court fashions would apparently permit a warrantless search of a passenger's briefcase if there is probable cause to believe the taxidriver had a syringe somewhere in his vehicle. . . .

Finally, in my view, the State's legitimate interest in effective law enforcement does not outweigh the privacy concerns at issue. I am as confident in a police officer's ability to apply a rule requiring a warrant or individualized probable cause to search belongings that are—as in this case—obviously owned by and in the custody of a passenger as is the Court in a "passenger-confederate[']s" ability to circumvent the rule. Certainly the ostensible clarity of the Court's rule is attractive. But that virtue is insufficient justification for its adoption. Moreover, a rule requiring a warrant or individualized probable cause to search passenger belongings is every bit as simple as the Court's rule; it simply protects more privacy.

## *Florida v. White*
### 119 S.Ct. 1555 (1999)

The facts are discussed by Justice Thomas in the opinion for the Court, reversing a decision of the Florida State Supreme Court. The Court's decision was seven to two, with Justice Souter filing a concurring opinion and Justice Stevens filing a dissenting opinion, which Justice Ginsburg joined.

Justice THOMAS delivered the opinion of the Court.

The Florida Contraband Forfeiture Act provides that certain forms of contraband, including motor vehicles used in violation of the Act's provisions, may be seized and potentially forfeited. In this case, we must decide whether the Fourth Amendment requires the police to obtain a warrant before seizing an automobile from a public place when they have probable cause to believe that it is forfeitable contraband. We hold that it does not.

On three occasions in July and August 1993, police officers observed respondent Tyvessel Tyvorus White using his car to deliver cocaine, and thereby developed probable cause to believe that his car was subject to forfeiture under the Florida Contraband Forfeiture Act. Several months later, the police arrested respondent at his place of employment on charges unrelated to the drug transactions observed in July and August 1993. At the same time, the arresting officers, without securing a warrant, seized respondent's automobile in accordance with the provisions of the Act. They seized the vehicle solely because they believed that it was forfeitable under the Act. During a subsequent inventory search, the police found two pieces of crack cocaine in the ashtray. Based on the discovery of the cocaine, respondent was charged with possession of a controlled substance in violation of Florida law.

At his trial on the possession charge, respondent filed a motion to suppress the evidence discovered during the inventory search. He argued that the warrantless seizure of his car violated the Fourth Amendment, thereby making the cocaine the "fruit of the poisonous tree." The trial court initially reserved ruling on respondent's motion, but later denied it after the jury returned a guilty verdict. On appeal, the Florida First District Court of Appeal affirmed. . . . Because the Florida Supreme Court and this Court had not directly addressed the issue, the court certified to the Florida Supreme Court the question whether, absent exigent circumstances, the warrantless seizure of an automobile under the Act violated the Fourth Amendment.

In a divided opinion, the Florida Supreme Court answered the certified question in the affirmative, quashed the First District Court of Appeal's opinion, and remanded. The majority of the court concluded that, absent exigent circumstances, the Fourth Amendment requires the police to obtain a warrant prior to seizing property that has been used in violation of the Act. . . . We granted *certiorari* and now reverse. . . .

In deciding whether a challenged governmental action violates the Amendment, we have taken care to inquire whether the action was regarded as an unlawful search and seizure when the Amendment was framed. See *Wyoming v. Houghton*, [119 S.Ct. 1297] (1999); *Carroll v. United States*, 267 U.S. 132 (1925).

In *Carroll*, we held that when federal officers have probable cause to believe that an automobile contains contraband, the Fourth Amendment does not require them to obtain a warrant prior to searching the car for and seizing the contraband. Our holding was rooted in federal law enforcement practice at the time of the adoption of the Fourth Amendment. Specifically, we looked to laws of the First, Second, and Fourth Congresses that authorized federal officers to conduct warrantless searches of ships and to seize concealed goods subject to duties. These enactments led us to conclude that "contemporaneously with the adoption of the Fourth Amendment," Congress distinguished "the necessity for a search warrant between goods subject to forfeiture, when concealed in a dwelling house or similar place, and like goods in course of transportation and concealed in a movable vessel where they readily could be put out of reach of a search warrant." . . .

In addition to the special considerations recognized in the context of movable items, our Fourth Amendment jurisprudence has consistently accorded law enforcement officials greater latitude in exercising their duties in public places. . . . Indeed, the facts of this case are nearly indistinguishable from those in *G. M. Leasing Corp. v. United States*, 429 U.S. 338 (1977). There, we considered whether federal agents violated the Fourth Amendment by failing to secure a warrant prior to seizing automobiles in partial satisfaction of income tax assessments. We concluded that they did not, reasoning that "[t]he seizures of the automobiles in this case took place on public streets, parking lots, or other open places, and did not involve any invasion of privacy." Here, because the police seized respondent's vehicle from a public area—respondent's employer's parking lot—the warrantless seizure also did not involve any invasion of respondent's privacy. . . .

The judgment of the Florida Supreme Court is reversed, and the case is remanded for proceedings not inconsistent with this opinion.


Justice STEVENS, with whom Justice GINSBURG joins, dissenting.


Because the Fourth Amendment plainly "protects property as well as privacy" and seizures as well as searches, I would apply to the present case our long-standing warrant presumption. In the context of property seizures by law enforcement authorities, the presumption might be overcome more easily in the absence of an accompanying privacy or liberty interest. Nevertheless, I would look to the warrant clause as a measure of reasonableness in such cases, and the circumstances of this case do not convince me that the role of a neutral magistrate was dispensable. . . .

Were we confronted with property that Florida deemed unlawful for private citizens to possess regardless of purpose, and had the State relied on the plain-view doctrine, perhaps a warrantless seizure would have been defensible. But "[t]here is nothing even remotely criminal in possessing an automobile," *Austin v. United States*, 509 U.S. 602 (1993); no serious fear for officer safety or loss of evidence can be asserted in this case considering the delay and circumstances of the seizure; and only the automobile exception is at issue. . . .

# 8

---

# THE FIFTH AMENDMENT GUARANTEE AGAINST SELF-ACCUSATION

## A. COERCED CONFESSIONS AND POLICE INTERROGATIONS

In a widely watched case, *Dickerson v. United States* (excerpted below), the Court reaffirmed the constitutionality of its ruling in *Miranda v. Arizona*, 384 U.S. 436 (1966) (in Vol. 2, Ch. 8), in holding that Congress could not override the decision by statute.

## *Dickerson v. United States*
### 120 S.Ct. 2326 (2000)

In *Miranda v. Arizona*, 384 U.S. 436 (1966) (see Vol. 2, Ch. 8), the Supreme Court held that, before police question criminal suspects, they must warn them of their Fifth and Sixth Amendment rights to remain silent and to have an attorney present; otherwise, any incriminating statements are considered involuntary and excluded at trial. That decision applied to all state courts and remains controversial. Two years later, Congress enacted the Crime Control and Safe Streets Act of 1968, in which Section 3501 specified that the pre-*Miranda* standard of "the totality of circumstances" for determining the voluntariness of a confession would apply in federal courts, not whether a defendant had been given the *Miranda* warnings. Subsequently, the Department of Justice, in both Republican and Democratic administrations, except in a couple of cases during the administration of Republican President Ronald Reagan, maintained the position that *Miranda* governed in both state and federal criminal prosecutions.

In 1997 Thomas Dickerson was arrested and indicted for bank robbery. At a pretrial hearing, his attorney moved to suppress an incriminating statement made at a Federal Bureau of Investigation office on the ground that the agents failed to read Dickerson his *Miranda* rights. A federal district court agreed that *Miranda* applied, but the Court of Appeals for the Fourth Circuit reversed, holding that *Miranda* was not a constitutional ruling and therefore Congress could determine the standard for voluntary confessions admitted into evidence in federal courts. That decision was appealed, and the Supreme Court granted review.

The appellate court's decision was reversed in a seven to two decision, and opinion for the Court was delivered by Chief Justice Rehnquist. Justice Scalia filed a dissenting opinion, which Justice Thomas joined.

Chief Justice REHNQUIST delivered the opinion of the Court.

We hold that *Miranda*, being a constitutional decision of this Court, may not be in effect overruled by an Act of Congress, and we decline to overrule *Miranda* ourselves. We therefore hold that *Miranda* and its progeny in this Court govern the admissibility of statements made during custodial interrogation in both state and federal courts. . . .

In *Miranda*, we noted that the advent of modern custodial police interrogation brought with it an increased concern about confessions obtained by coercion. Because custodial police interrogation, by its very nature, isolates and pressures the individual, we stated that "[e]ven without employing brutality, the 'third degree' or [other] specific stratagems, custodial interrogation exacts a heavy toll on individual liberty and trades on the weakness of individuals." We concluded that the coercion inherent in custodial interrogation blurs the line between voluntary and involuntary statements, and thus heightens the risk that an individual will not be "accorded his privilege under the Fifth Amendment not to be compelled to incriminate himself." Accordingly, we laid down "concrete constitutional guidelines for law enforcement agencies and courts to follow." Those guidelines established that the admissibility in evidence of any statement given during custodial interrogation of a suspect would depend on whether the police provided the suspect with four warnings. These warnings (which have come to be known colloquially as *Miranda* rights") are: a suspect "has the right to remain silent, that anything he says can be used against him in a court of law, that he has the right to the presence of an attorney, and that if he cannot afford an attorney one will be appointed for him prior to any questioning if he so desires."

Two years after *Miranda* was decided, Congress enacted Section 3501. Given Section 3501's express designation of voluntariness as the touchstone of admissibility, its omission of any warning requirement, and the instruction for trial courts to consider a nonexclusive list of factors relevant to the circumstances of a confession, we agree with the Court of Appeals that Congress intended by its enactment to overrule *Miranda*. Because of the obvious conflict between our decision in *Miranda* and Section 3501, we must address whether Congress has constitutional authority to thus supersede *Miranda*. If Congress has such authority, Section 3501's totality-of-the-circumstances approach must prevail over *Miranda*'s requirement of warnings; if not, that section must yield to *Miranda*'s more specific requirements.

The law in this area is clear. This Court has supervisory authority over the federal courts, and we may use that authority to prescribe rules of evidence and procedure that are binding in those tribunals. However, the power to judicially create and enforce nonconstitutional "rules of procedure and evidence for the federal courts exists only in the absence of a relevant Act of Congress." Congress retains the ultimate authority to modify or set aside any judicially created rules of evidence and procedure that are not required by the Constitution.

But Congress may not legislatively supersede our decisions interpreting and applying the Constitution. See, e.g., *City of Boerne v. Flores*, 521 U.S. 507 (1997). This case therefore turns on whether the *Miranda* Court announced a constitutional rule or merely exercised its supervisory authority to regulate evidence in the absence of congressional direction. Recognizing this point, the Court of Appeals surveyed *Miranda* and its progeny to determine the constitutional status of the *Miranda* decision. Relying on the fact that we have created several exceptions to *Miranda*'s warnings requirement and that we have repeatedly referred to the *Miranda* warnings as "prophylactic," *New York v. Quarles*, 467 U.S. 649 (1984), and "not themselves rights protected by the Constitution," *Michigan v. Tucker*, 417 U.S. 433 (1974), the Court of Appeals concluded that the protections announced in *Miranda* are not constitutionally required.

We disagree with the Court of Appeals' conclusion, although we concede that there is language in some of our opinions that supports the view taken by that court. But first and foremost of the factors on the other side—that *Miranda* is a constitutional decision—is that both *Miranda* and two of its companion cases applied the rule to proceedings in state courts—to wit, Arizona, California, and New York. Since that time, we have consistently applied *Miranda*'s rule to prosecutions arising in state courts. It is beyond dispute that we do not hold a supervisory power over the courts of the several States.

The *Miranda* opinion itself begins by stating that the Court granted *certiorari* "to explore some facets of the problems of applying the privilege against self-incrimination to in-custody interrogation, and to give concrete constitutional guidelines for law enforcement agencies and courts to follow." In fact, the majority opinion is replete with statements indicating that the majority thought it was announcing a constitutional rule. Indeed, the Court's ultimate conclusion was that the unwarned confessions obtained in the four cases before the Court in *Miranda* "were obtained from the defendant under circumstances that did not meet constitutional standards for protection of the privilege."

The dissent argues that it is judicial overreaching for this Court to hold Section 3501 unconstitutional unless we hold that the *Miranda* warnings are required by the Constitution, in the sense that nothing else will suffice to satisfy constitutional requirements. But we need not go farther than *Miranda* to decide this case. In *Miranda*, the Court noted that reliance on the traditional totality-of-the-circumstances test raised a risk of overlooking an involuntary custodial confession, a risk that the Court found unacceptably great when the confession is offered in the case in chief to prove guilt. The Court therefore concluded that something more than the totality test was necessary. As discussed above, Section 3501 reinstates the totality test as sufficient. Section 3501 therefore cannot be sustained if *Miranda* is to remain the law.

Whether or not we would agree with *Miranda*'s reasoning and its resulting rule, were we addressing the issue in the first instance, the principles of *stare decisis* weigh heavily against overruling it now.

We do not think there is such justification for overruling *Miranda*. *Miranda* has become embedded in routine police practice to the point where the warnings have become part of our national culture. See *Mitchell v. United States*, 526 U.S. 314 (1999) (SCALIA, J., dissenting) (stating that the fact that a rule has found "wide acceptance in the legal culture" is "adequate reason not to overrule" it). While we have overruled our precedents when subsequent cases have undermined their doctrinal underpinnings, we do not believe that this has happened to the *Miranda* decision. If anything, our subsequent cases have reduced the impact of the *Miranda* rule on legitimate law enforcement while reaffirming the decision's core ruling that unwarned statements may not be used as evidence in the prosecution's case in chief.

The disadvantage of the *Miranda* rule is that statements which may be by no means involuntary, made by a defendant who is aware of his "rights," may nonetheless be excluded and a guilty defendant go free as a result. But experience suggests that the totality-of-the-circumstances test which Section 3501 seeks to revive is more difficult than *Miranda* for law enforcement officers to conform to, and for courts to apply in a consistent manner. The requirement that *Miranda* warnings be given does not, of course, dispense with the voluntariness inquiry. But as we said in *Berkemer v. McCarty*, 468 U.S. 420 (1984), "[c]ases in which a defendant can make a colorable argument that a self-incriminating statement was 'compelled' despite the fact that the law enforcement authorities adhered to the dictates of *Miranda* are rare."

In sum, we conclude that *Miranda* announced a constitutional rule that Congress may not supersede legislatively. Following the rule of *stare decisis*, we decline to overrule *Miranda* ourselves. The judgment of the Court of Appeals is therefore Reversed.

Justice SCALIA, with whom Justice THOMAS joins, dissenting.

Those to whom judicial decisions are an unconnected series of judgments that produce either favored or disfavored results will doubtless greet today's decision as a paragon of moderation, since it declines to overrule *Miranda v. Arizona*. Those who understand the judicial process will appreciate that today's decision is not a reaffirmation of *Miranda*, but a radical revision of the most significant element of *Miranda* (as of all cases): the rationale that gives it a permanent place in our jurisprudence.

*Marbury v. Madison*, 1 Cranch 137 (1803), held that an Act of Congress will not be enforced by the courts if what it prescribes violates the Constitution of the United States. That was the basis on which *Miranda* was decided. One will search today's opinion in vain, however, for a statement (surely simple enough to make) that what Section 3501 prescribes—the use at trial of a voluntary confession, even when a *Miranda* warning or its equivalent has failed to be given— violates the Constitution. The reason the statement does not appear is not only (and perhaps not so much) that it would be absurd, inasmuch as Section 3501 excludes from trial precisely what the Constitution excludes from trial, viz., compelled confessions; but also that Justices whose votes are needed to compose today's majority are on record as believing that a violation of *Miranda* is not a violation of the Constitution. And so, to justify today's agreed-upon result, the Court must adopt a significant new, if not entirely comprehensible, principle of constitutional law. As the Court chooses to describe that principle, statutes of Congress can be disregarded, not only when what they prescribe violates the Constitution, but when what they prescribe contradicts a decision of this Court that "announced a constitutional rule." As I shall discuss in some detail, the only thing that can possibly mean in the context of this case is that this Court has the power, not merely to apply the Constitution but to expand it, imposing what it regards as useful "prophylactic" restrictions upon Congress and the States. That is an immense and frightening antidemocratic power, and it does not exist.

It takes only a small step to bring today's opinion out of the realm of power-judging and into the mainstream of legal reasoning: The Court need only go beyond its carefully couched iterations that "*Miranda* is a constitutional decision," that "*Miranda* is constitutionally based," that *Miranda* has "constitutional underpinnings," and come out and say quite clearly: "We reaffirm today that custodial interrogation that is not preceded by *Miranda* warnings or their equivalent violates the Constitution of the United States." It cannot say that, because a majority of the Court does not believe it. The Court therefore acts in plain violation of the Constitution when it denies effect to this Act of Congress.

It was once possible to characterize the so-called *Miranda* rule as resting (however implausibly) upon the proposition that what the statute here before us permits—the admission at trial of un-Mirandized confessions—violates the Constitution. That is the fairest reading of the *Miranda* case itself. The Court began by announcing that the Fifth Amendment privilege against self-incrimination applied in the context of extrajudicial custodial interrogation—itself a doubtful proposition as a matter both of history and precedent. Having extended the privilege into the confines of the station house, the Court liberally sprinkled throughout its sprawling 60-page opinion suggestions that, because of the compulsion inherent in custodial interrogation, the privilege was violated by any statement thus obtained that did not conform to the rules set forth in *Miranda*, or some functional equivalent. . . .

*Miranda* was objectionable for innumerable reasons, not least the fact that cases spanning more than 70 years had rejected its core premise that, absent the warnings and an effective waiver of the right to remain silent and of the (thitherto unknown) right to have an attorney present, a statement obtained pursuant to custodial interrogation was necessarily the product of compulsion. Moreover, history and precedent aside, the decision in *Miranda*, if read as an explication of what the Constitution requires, is preposterous. There is, for example, simply no basis in reason for concluding that a response to the very first question asked, by a suspect who already knows all of the rights described in the *Miranda* warning, is anything other than a volitional act. And even if one assumes that the elimination of compulsion absolutely requires informing even the most knowledgeable suspect of his right to remain silent, it cannot conceivably require the right to have counsel present. There is a world of difference, which the Court recognized under the traditional voluntariness test but ignored in *Miranda*, between compelling a suspect to incriminate himself and preventing him from foolishly doing so of his own accord. Only the latter (which is not required by the Constitution) could explain the Court's inclusion of a right to counsel and the requirement that it, too, be knowingly and intelligently waived. Counsel's presence is not required to tell the suspect that he need not speak; the interrogators can do that. The only good reason for having counsel there is that he can be counted on to advise the suspect that he should not speak.

Preventing foolish (rather than compelled) confessions is likewise the only conceivable basis for the rules that courts must exclude any confession elicited by questioning conducted, without interruption, after the suspect has indicated a desire to stand on his right to remain silent, see *Michigan v. Mosley*, 423 U.S. 96 (1975), or initiated by police after the suspect has expressed a desire to have counsel present, see *Edwards v. Arizona*, 451 U.S. 477 (1981). Nonthreatening attempts to persuade the suspect to reconsider that initial decision are not, without more, enough to render a change of heart the product of anything other than the suspect's free will. Thus, what is most remarkable about the *Miranda* decision—and what made it unacceptable as a matter of straightforward constitutional interpretation in the *Marbury* tradition—is its palpable hostility toward the act of confession per se, rather than toward what the Constitution abhors, compelled confession.

For these reasons, and others more than adequately developed in the *Miranda* dissents and in the subsequent works of the decision's many critics, any conclusion that a violation of the *Miranda* rules necessarily amounts to a violation of the privilege against compelled self-incrimination can claim no support in history, precedent, or common sense, and as a result would at least presumptively be worth reconsidering even at this late date. But that is unnecessary, since the Court has (thankfully) long since abandoned the notion that failure to comply with *Miranda*'s rules is itself a violation of the Constitution.

As the Court today acknowledges, since *Miranda* we have explicitly, and repeatedly, interpreted that decision as having announced, not the circumstances in which custodial interrogation runs afoul of the Fifth or Fourteenth Amendment, but rather only "prophylactic" rules that go beyond the right against compelled self-incrimination. Of course the seeds of this "prophylactic" interpretation of *Miranda* were present in the decision itself. In subsequent cases, the seeds have sprouted and borne fruit: The Court has squarely concluded that it is possible—indeed not uncommon—for the police to violate *Miranda* without also violating the Constitution. [See, *Michigan v. Tucker*, 417 U.S. 433 (1974); *Oregon v. Hass*, 420 U.S. 714 (1975); *New York v. Quarles*, 467 U.S. 649 (1984); and *Oregon v. Elstad*, 470 U.S. 298 (1985).]

In light of these cases, and our statements to the same effect in others, it is simply no longer possible for the Court to conclude, even if it wanted to, that a violation of *Miranda*'s rules is a violation of the Constitution. But as I explained at the outset, that is what is required before the Court may disregard a law of Congress governing the admissibility of evidence in federal court. The Court today insists that the decision in *Miranda* is a "constitutional" one; that it has "constitutional underpinnings"; "constitutional basis" and a "constitutional origin"; that it was "constitutionally based"; and that it announced a "constitutional rule." It is fine to play these word games; but what makes a decision "constitutional" in the only sense relevant here—in the sense that renders it impervious to supersession by congressional legislation such as Section 3501—is the determination that the Constitution requires the result that the decision announces and the statute ignores. By disregarding congressional action that concededly does not violate the Constitution, the Court flagrantly offends fundamental principles of separation of powers, and arrogates to itself prerogatives reserved to the representatives of the people. . . .

Despite the Court's Orwellian assertion to the contrary, it is undeniable that later cases (discussed above) have "undermined [*Miranda*'s] doctrinal underpinnings," denying constitutional violation and thus stripping the holding of its only constitutionally legitimate support.

Neither am I persuaded by the argument for retaining *Miranda* that touts its supposed workability as compared with the totality-of-the-circumstances test it purported to replace. *Miranda*'s proponents cite ad nauseam the fact that the Court was called upon to make difficult and subtle distinctions in applying the "voluntariness" test in some 30-odd due process "coerced confessions" cases in the 30 years between *Brown v. Mississippi,* 297 U.S. 278 (1936), and *Miranda.* It is not immediately apparent, however, that the judicial burden has been eased by the "bright-line" rules adopted in *Miranda.* In fact, in the 34 years since *Miranda* was decided, this Court has been called upon to decide nearly 60 cases involving a host of *Miranda* issues, most of them predicted with remarkable prescience by Justice WHITE in his *Miranda* dissent. . . .

Finally, I am not convinced by petitioner's argument that *Miranda* should be preserved because the decision occupies a special place in the "public's consciousness." As far as I am aware, the public is not under the illusion that we are infallible. I see little harm in admitting that we made a mistake in taking away from the people the ability to decide for themselves what protections (beyond those required by the Constitution) are reasonably affordable in the criminal investigatory process. And I see much to be gained by reaffirming for the people the wonderful reality that they govern themselves—which means that "[t]he powers not delegated to the United States by the Constitution" that the people adopted, "nor prohibited to the States" by that Constitution, "are reserved to the States respectively, or to the people," U.S. Const., Amdt. 10. . . .

I dissent from today's decision, and, until Section 3501 is repealed, will continue to apply it in all cases where there has been a sustainable finding that the defendant's confession was voluntary.

# 9

---

# THE RIGHTS TO COUNSEL
# AND OTHER PROCEDURAL
# GUARANTEES

## A. THE RIGHT TO COUNSEL

In *Martinez v. Court of Appeal of California*, 120 S.Ct. 684 (2000), the Court held that the Sixth Amendment right to waive the benefits of counsel and to self-representation at trials, recognized in *Faretta v. California*, 422 U.S. 806 (1975), does not extend to direct appeals of criminal convictions. In writing for the Court, Justice Stevens reaffirmed that the Sixth Amendment right to self-representation does not apply to appellate proceedings.

## B. PLEA BARGAINING AND THE RIGHT
## TO EFFECTIVE COUNSEL

---

### THE DEVELOPMENT OF LAW

### Rulings on Plea Bargaining and Effective Counsel

| Case | Vote | Ruling |
|------|------|--------|
| *Roe v. Flores-Ortega*, 120 S.Ct. 1029 (2000) | 6:3 | Writing for the Court, Justice O'Connor reaffirmed the holding, in *Strickland v. Washington*, 466 U.S. 668 (1984), that a defendant claiming ineffective counsel must show (1) that the counsel's representation fell below an objective standard of reasonableness and (2) that the deficient performance prejudiced the defendant. It was further held that counsel has a constitutionally imposed duty to consult with the defendant about an appeal when there is reason to think either that a rational defendant would want to appeal or that the defendant indicated an interest in appealing. |

---

*Williams v. Taylor*, 120 S.Ct. 1495 (2000)    6:3 and 5:4    Writing for the Court, Justice Stevens held that Terry Williams was denied his constitutionally guaranteed right to effective counsel, as defined in *Strickland v. Washington*, 466 U.S. 668 (1984), because his attorney failed to investigate and to present substantial mitigating evidence to the jury, and thus he was entitled to appeal his death sentence under the Antiterrorism and Effective Death Penalty Act of 1996 (AEDPA). Justices O'Connor, Kennedy, Souter, Ginsburg, and Breyer joined portions of the opinion. Justice O'Connor delivered the opinion of the Court, holding that the AEDPA places a new constraint on federal courts in granting writs of *habeas corpus* review; they may grant review only if the state court's adjudication was "contrary to" or "involved an unreasonable application of clearly established federal law." Chief Justice Rehnquist and Justices Kennedy, Scalia, and Thomas joined that opinion.

# 10

# CRUEL AND UNUSUAL PUNISHMENT

## B. CAPITAL PUNISHMENT

---

### THE DEVELOPMENT OF LAW

#### Post-*Furman* Rulings
#### on Capital Punishment

| Case | Vote | Ruling |
|------|------|--------|
| *Williams v. Taylor*, 120 S.Ct. 1479 (2000) | 9:0 | Justice Kennedy held that, under the Antiterrorism and Effective Death Penalty Act |

of 1996, which limits federal court *habeas* review, Michael Williams and other death row inmates may raise issues in federal appeals for which they were unable to develop enough information to bring up during state court proceedings, if they were diligent in seeking the information.

| *Williams v. Taylor*, 120 S.Ct. 1495 (2000) | 6:3 and 5:4 | Writing for the Court, Justice Stevens held that Terry Williams was denied his con- |

stitutionally guaranteed right to effective counsel, as defined in *Strickland v. Washington*, 466 U.S. 668 (1984), because his attorney failed to investigate and to present substantial mitigating evidence to the jury, and thus he was entitled to appeal his death sentence under the Antiterrorism and Effective Death Penalty Act of 1996 (AEDPA). Justices O'Connor, Kennedy, Souter, Ginsburg, and Breyer joined portions of the opinion. Justice O'Connor delivered the opinion of the Court, holding that the AEDPA places a new constraint on federal courts in granting writs of *habeas corpus* review; they may grant review only if the state court's adjudication was "contrary to" or "involved an unreasonable application of clearly established federal law." Chief Justice Rehnquist and Justices Kennedy, Scalia, and Thomas joined that opinion.

---

*Ramdass v. Angelone,*   5:4   Justice Kennedy held that
120 S.Ct. 2113 (2000)   the failure to inform the sentencing jury in a capital case
that the defendant was not entitled to parole under Virginia's "three strikes
and you're out" law, which denies parole for those convicted of three separate felonies, did not run afoul of constitutional requirements. Justices
Stevens, Souter, Ginsburg, and Breyer dissented.

# 11

---

# THE RIGHT OF PRIVACY

## A. PRIVACY AND REPRODUCTIVE FREEDOM

For the first time since *Planned Parenthood of Southeastern Pennsylvania v. Casey*, 505 U.S. 833 (1992) (excerpted in Vol. 2, Ch. 11), the Court handed down a ruling on abortion in *Stenberg v. Carhart* (excerpted below). By a five to four vote, the Court struck down Nebraska's ban on "partial birth abortions" as an "undue burden" on women.

## Stenberg v. Carhart
### 120 S.Ct. 2597 (2000)

The Court's decision was five to four in affirming the federal appellate court's decision invalidating Nebraska's "partial birth abortion" law. The facts are discussed in the opinion for the Court delivered by Justice Breyer. Justices Ginsburg and Stevens filed concurring opinions. Chief Justice Rehnquist and Justices Kennedy, Scalia, and Thomas each filed dissenting opinions.

Justice BREYER delivered the opinion of the Court.

We again consider the right to an abortion. We understand the controversial nature of the problem. Millions of Americans believe that life begins at conception and consequently that an abortion is akin to causing the death of an innocent child; they recoil at the thought of a law that would permit it. Other millions fear that a law that forbids abortion would condemn many American women to lives that lack dignity, depriving them of equal liberty and leading those with least resources to undergo illegal abortions with the attendant risks of death and suffering. Taking account of these virtually irreconcilable points of view, aware that constitutional law must govern a society whose different members sincerely hold directly opposing views, and considering the matter in light of the Constitution's guarantees of fundamental individual liberty, this Court, in the course of a generation, has determined and then redetermined that the Constitution offers basic protection to the woman's right to choose. *Roe v. Wade*, 410 U.S. 113 (1973); *Planned Parenthood of Southeastern Pa. v. Casey*, 505 U.S. 833 (1992). We shall not revisit those legal principles. Rather, we apply them to the circumstances of this case.

Three established principles determine the issue before us. We shall set them forth in the language of the joint opinion in *Casey*. First, before "viability the woman has a right to choose to terminate her pregnancy."

Second, "a law designed to further the State's interest in fetal life which imposes an undue burden on the woman's decision before fetal viability" is unconstitutional. An "undue burden is shorthand for the conclusion that a state regulation has the purpose or effect of placing a substantial obstacle in the path of a woman seeking an abortion of a nonviable fetus."

Third, "subsequent to viability, the State in promoting its interest in the potentiality of human life may, if it chooses, regulate, and even proscribe, abortion except where it is necessary, in appropriate medical judgment, for the preservation of the life or health of the mother."

We apply these principles to a Nebraska law banning "partial birth abortion." The statute reads as follows: "No partial birth abortion shall be performed in this state, unless such procedure is necessary to save the life of the mother whose life is endangered by a physical disorder, physical illness, or physical injury, including a life-endangering physical condition caused by or arising from the pregnancy itself." The statute defines "partial birth abortion" as: "an abortion procedure in which the person performing the abortion partially delivers vaginally a living unborn child before killing the unborn child and completing the delivery." It further defines "partially delivers vaginally a living unborn child before killing the unborn child" to mean "deliberately and intentionally delivering into the vagina a living unborn child, or a substantial portion thereof, for the purpose of performing a procedure that the person performing such procedure knows will kill the unborn child and does kill the unborn child." The law classifies violation of the statute as a "Class III felony" carrying a prison term of up to 20 years, and a fine of up to $25,000. It also provides for the automatic revocation of a doctor's license to practice medicine in Nebraska.

We hold that this statute violates the Constitution. . . .

The evidence before the trial court, as supported or supplemented in the literature, indicates the following:

1. About 90% of all abortions performed in the United States take place during the first trimester of pregnancy, before 12 weeks of gestational age. During the first trimester, the predominant abortion method is "vacuum aspiration," which involves insertion of a vacuum tube (cannula) into the uterus to evacuate the contents. Such an abortion is typically performed on an outpatient basis under local anesthesia. The procedure's mortality rates for first trimester abortion are, for example, 5 to 10 times lower than those associated with carrying the fetus to term. Complication rates are also low. As the fetus grows in size, however, the vacuum aspiration method becomes increasingly difficult to use.

2. Approximately 10% of all abortions are performed during the second trimester of pregnancy (12 to 24 weeks). In the early 1970's, inducing labor through the injection of saline into the uterus was the predominant method of second trimester abortion. Today, however, the medical profession has switched from medical induction of labor to surgical procedures for most second trimester

abortions. The most commonly used procedure is called "dilation and evacuation" (D&E). That procedure (together with a modified form of vacuum aspiration used in the early second trimester) accounts for about 95% of all abortions performed from 12 to 20 weeks of gestational age.

3. D&E "refers generically to transcervical procedures performed at 13 weeks gestation or later." . . . There are variations in D&E operative strategy. However, the common points are that D&E involves (1) dilation of the cervix; (2) removal of at least some fetal tissue using nonvacuum instruments; and (3) (after the 15th week) the potential need for instrumental disarticulation or dismemberment of the fetus or the collapse of fetal parts to facilitate evacuation from the uterus.

4. When instrumental disarticulation incident to D&E is necessary, it typically occurs as the doctor pulls a portion of the fetus through the cervix into the birth canal. . . .

5. The D&E procedure carries certain risks. The use of instruments within the uterus creates a danger of accidental perforation and damage to neighboring organs. Sharp fetal bone fragments create similar dangers. And fetal tissue accidentally left behind can cause infection and various other complications. Nonetheless studies show that the risks of mortality and complication that accompany the D&E procedure between the 12th and 20th weeks of gestation are significantly lower than those accompanying induced labor procedures (the next safest midsecond trimester procedures).

6. At trial, Dr. Carhart and Dr. Stubblefield described a variation of the D&E procedure, which they referred to as an "intact D&E." Like other versions of the D&E technique, it begins with induced dilation of the cervix. The procedure then involves removing the fetus from the uterus through the cervix "intact," i.e., in one pass, rather than in several passes. It is used after 16 weeks at the earliest, as vacuum aspiration becomes ineffective and the fetal skull becomes too large to pass through the cervix. . . .

7. The intact D&E procedure can also be found described in certain obstetric and abortion clinical textbooks, where two variations are recognized. The first, as just described, calls for the physician to adapt his method for extracting the intact fetus depending on fetal presentation. A slightly different version of the intact D&E procedure, associated with Dr. Martin Haskell, calls for conversion to a breech presentation in all cases.

8. The American College of Obstetricians and Gynecologists describes the D&X procedure in a manner corresponding to a breech-conversion intact D&E, including the following steps: "1. deliberate dilatation of the cervix, usually over a sequence of days; 2. instrumental conversion of the fetus to a footling breech; 3. breech extraction of the body excepting the head; and 4. partial evacuation of the intracranial contents of a living fetus to effect vaginal delivery of a dead but otherwise intact fetus." Despite the technical differences we have just described, intact D&E and D&X are sufficiently similar for us to use the terms interchangeably.

9. Dr. Carhart testified he attempts to use the intact D&E procedure during weeks 16 to 20 because (1) it reduces the dangers from sharp bone fragments passing through the cervix, (2) minimizes the number of instrument passes needed for extraction and lessens the likelihood of uterine perforations caused by those instruments, (3) reduces the likelihood of leaving infection-causing fetal and placental tissue in the uterus, and (4) could help to prevent potentially fatal absorption of fetal tissue into the maternal circulation. The District Court

made no findings about the D&X procedure's overall safety. The District Court concluded, however, that "the evidence is both clear and convincing that Carhart's D&X procedure is superior to, and safer than, the other abortion procedures used during the relevant gestational period in the 10 to 20 cases a year that present to Dr. Carhart."

10. The materials presented at trial referred to the potential benefits of the D&X procedure in circumstances involving nonviable fetuses, such as fetuses with abnormal fluid accumulation in the brain (hydrocephaly).

11. There are no reliable data on the number of D&X abortions performed annually. Estimates have ranged between 640 and 5,000 per year.

The question before us is whether Nebraska's statute, making criminal the performance of a "partial birth abortion," violates the Federal Constitution, as interpreted in *Planned Parenthood of Southeastern Pa. v. Casey*, and *Roe v. Wade*. We conclude that it does for at least two independent reasons. First, the law lacks any exception "for the preservation of the health of the mother." Second, it "imposes an undue burden on a woman's ability" to choose a D&E abortion, thereby unduly burdening the right to choose abortion itself. We shall discuss each of these reasons in turn. . . .

The fact that Nebraska's law applies both pre- and postviability aggravates the constitutional problem presented. The State's interest in regulating abortion previability is considerably weaker than postviability. Since the law requires a health exception in order to validate even a postviability abortion regulation, it at a minimum requires the same in respect to previability regulation.

The quoted standard also depends on the state regulations "promoting [the State's] interest in the potentiality of human life." The Nebraska law, of course, does not directly further an interest "in the potentiality of human life" by saving the fetus in question from destruction, as it regulates only a method of performing abortion. Nebraska describes its interests differently. It says the law "show[s] concern for the life of the unborn," "prevent[s] cruelty to partially born children," and "preserve[s] the integrity of the medical profession." But we cannot see how the interest-related differences could make any difference to the question at hand, namely, the application of the "health" requirement.

Consequently, the governing standard requires an exception "where it is necessary, in appropriate medical judgment for the preservation of the life or health of the mother," for this Court has made clear that a State may promote but not endanger a woman's health when it regulates the methods of abortion. *Thornburgh v. American College of Obstetricians and Gynecologists*, 476 U.S. 747 (1986); *Colautti v. Franklin*, 439 U.S. 379 (1979); *Doe v. Bolton*, 410 U.S. 179 (1973). Justice THOMAS says that the cases just cited limit this principle to situations where the pregnancy itself creates a threat to health. He is wrong. The cited cases, reaffirmed in *Casey*, recognize that a State cannot subject women's health to significant risks both in that context, and also where state regulations force women to use riskier methods of abortion. Our cases have repeatedly invalidated statutes that in the process of regulating the methods of abortion, imposed significant health risks. They make clear that a risk to a women's health is the same whether it happens to arise from regulating a particular method of abortion, or from barring abortion entirely. Our holding does not go beyond those cases, as ratified in *Casey*. . . .

Nebraska responds that the law does not require a health exception unless there is a need for such an exception. . . . Nebraska, along with supporting *amici*, replies that these findings are irrelevant, wrong, or applicable only in a tiny number of instances. It says (1) that the D&X procedure is "little-used," (2) by only "a handful of doctors." It argues (3) that D&E and labor induction are at all times "safe alternative procedures." It refers to the testimony of petitioners' medical expert, who testified (4) that the ban would not increase a woman's risk of several rare abortion complications (disseminated intravascular coagulopathy and amniotic fluid embolus).

The Association of American Physicians and Surgeons et al., *amici* supporting Nebraska, argue (5) that elements of the D&X procedure may create special risks, including cervical incompetence caused by overdilitation, injury caused by conversion of the fetal presentation, and dangers arising from the "blind" use of instrumentation to pierce the fetal skull while lodged in the birth canal.

Nebraska further emphasizes (6) that there are no medical studies "establishing the safety of the partial-birth abortion/D&X procedure," and "no medical studies comparing the safety of partial-birth abortion/D&X to other abortion procedures," (7) an American Medical Association policy statement that "there does not appear to be any identified situation in which intact D&X is the only appropriate procedure to induce abortion." And it points out (8) that the American College of Obstetricians and Gynecologists qualified its statement that D&X "may be the best or most appropriate procedure," by adding that the panel "could identify no circumstances under which [the D&X] procedure would be the only option to save the life or preserve the health of the woman."

We find these eight arguments insufficient to demonstrate that Nebraska's law needs no health exception. For one thing, certain of the arguments are beside the point. The D&X procedure's relative rarity (argument (1)) is not highly relevant. The D&X is an infrequently used abortion procedure; but the health exception question is whether protecting women's health requires an exception for those infrequent occasions. A rarely used treatment might be necessary to treat a rarely occurring disease that could strike anyone—the State cannot prohibit a person from obtaining treatment simply by pointing out that most people do not need it. Nor can we know whether the fact that only a "handful" of doctors use the procedure (argument (2)) reflects the comparative rarity of late second term abortions, the procedure's recent development, the controversy surrounding it, or, as Nebraska suggests, the procedure's lack of utility.

For another thing, the record responds to Nebraska's (and *amici*'s) medically based arguments. In respect to argument (3), for example, the District Court agreed that alternatives, such as D&E and induced labor, are "safe" but found that the D&X method was significantly safer in certain circumstances. In respect to argument (4), the District Court simply relied on different expert testimony—testimony stating that "[a]nother advantage of the Intact D&E is that it eliminates the risk of embolism of cerebral tissue into the woman's blood stream."

In response to *amici*'s argument (5), the American College of Obstetricians and Gynecologists, in its own *amici* brief, denies that D&X generally poses risks greater than the alternatives. It says that the suggested alternative procedures involve similar or greater risks of cervical and uterine injury, for "D&E procedures, involve similar amounts of dilitation" and "of course childbirth involves even greater cervical dilitation." The College points out that Dr. Carhart does not reposition the fetus thereby avoiding any risks stemming from conversion to breech presentation, and that, as compared with D&X, D&E involves the same, if not greater, "blind" use of sharp instruments in the uterine cavity.

We do not quarrel with Nebraska's argument (6), for Nebraska is right. There are no general medical studies documenting comparative safety. Neither do we deny the import of the American Medical Association's statement (argument (7))—even though the State does omit the remainder of that statement: "The AMA recommends that the procedure not be used unless alternative procedures pose materially greater risk to the woman."

We cannot, however, read the American College of Obstetricians and Gynecologists panel's qualification (that it could not "identify" a circumstance where D&X was the "only" life- or health-preserving option) as if, according to Nebraska's argument (8), it denied the potential health-related need for D&X. That is because the College writes the following in its *amici* brief: "Depending on the physician's skill and experience, the D&X procedure can be the most appropriate abortion procedure for some women in some circumstances. D&X presents a variety of potential safety advantages over other abortion procedures used during the same gestational period." . . .

The upshot is a District Court finding that D&X significantly obviates health risks in certain circumstances, a highly plausible record-based explanation of why that might be so, a division of opinion among some medical experts over whether D&X is generally safer, and an absence of controlled medical studies that would help answer these medical questions. Given these medically related evidentiary circumstances, we believe the law requires a health exception. . . .

The Eighth Circuit found the Nebraska statute unconstitutional because, in *Casey*'s words, it has the "effect of placing a substantial obstacle in the path of a woman seeking an abortion of a nonviable fetus." It thereby places an "undue burden" upon a woman's right to terminate her pregnancy before viability. Nebraska does not deny that the statute imposes an "undue burden" if it applies to the more commonly used D&E procedure as well as to D&X. And we agree with the Eighth Circuit that it does so apply. . . .

The judgment of the Court of Appeals is affirmed.


Justice O'CONNOR, concurring.

I write separately to emphasize the following points.

First, the Nebraska statute is inconsistent with *Casey* because it lacks an exception for those instances when the banned procedure is necessary to preserve the health of the mother. . . . Contrary to the assertions of Justice KENNEDY and Justice THOMAS, the need for a health exception does not arise from "the individual views of Dr. Carhart and his supporters." Rather, as the majority explains, where, as here, "a significant body of medical opinion believes a procedure may bring with it greater safety for some patients and explains the medical reasons supporting that view," then Nebraska cannot say that the procedure will not, in some circumstances, be "necessary to preserve the life or health of the mother." Accordingly, our precedent requires that the statute include a health exception.

Second, Nebraska's statute is unconstitutional on the alternative and independent ground that it imposes an undue burden on a woman's right to choose to terminate her pregnancy before viability. Nebraska's ban covers not just the dilation and extraction (D&X) procedure, but also the dilation and evacuation

(D&E) procedure, "the most commonly used method for performing previability second trimester abortions." . . . Thus, it is not possible to interpret the statute's language as applying only to the D&X procedure. Moreover, it is significant that both the District Court and the Court of Appeals interpreted the statute as prohibiting abortions performed using the D&E method as well as the D&X method. . . . Indeed, Nebraska conceded at oral argument that "the State could not prohibit the D&E procedure." By proscribing the most commonly used method for previability second trimester abortions, the statute creates a "substantial obstacle to a woman seeking an abortion," and therefore imposes an undue burden on a woman's right to terminate her pregnancy prior to viability.

It is important to note that, unlike Nebraska, some other States have enacted statutes more narrowly tailored to proscribing the D&X procedure alone. Some of those statutes have done so by specifically excluding from their coverage the most common methods of abortion, such as the D&E and vacuum aspiration procedures. . . . By restricting their prohibitions to the D&X procedure exclusively, the Kansas, Utah, and Montana statutes avoid a principal defect of the Nebraska law. . . .

Nebraska's statute, however, does not meet these criteria. It contains no exception for when the procedure, in appropriate medical judgment, is necessary to preserve the health of the mother; and it proscribes not only the D&X procedure but also the D&E procedure, the most commonly used method for previability second trimester abortions, thus making it an undue burden on a woman's right to terminate her pregnancy. For these reasons, I agree with the Court that Nebraska's law is unconstitutional.

Justice GINSBURG, with whom Justice STEVENS joins, concurring.

I write separately only to stress that amidst all the emotional uproar caused by an abortion case, we should not lose sight of the character of Nebraska's "partial birth abortion" law. As the Court observes, this law does not save any fetus from destruction, for it targets only "a method of performing abortion." Nor does the statute seek to protect the lives or health of pregnant women. Moreover, as Justice STEVENS points out, the most common method of performing previability second trimester abortions is no less distressing or susceptible to gruesome description. . . .

A state regulation that "has the purpose or effect of placing a substantial obstacle in the path of a woman seeking an abortion of a nonviable fetus" violates the Constitution. *Casey.*

Justice STEVENS, with whom Justice GINSBURG joins, concurring.

[D]uring the past 27 years, the central holding of *Roe v. Wade* has been endorsed by all but 4 of the 17 Justices who have addressed the issue. That holding—that the word "liberty" in the Fourteenth Amendment includes a woman's right to make this difficult and extremely personal decision—makes it impossible for me to understand how a State has any legitimate interest in requiring a doctor to follow any procedure other than the one that he or she reasonably believes will best protect the woman in her exercise of this constitutional liberty. But one need not even approach this view today to conclude that Nebraska's law must fall. For the notion that either of these two equally gruesome procedures performed at this late stage of gestation is more akin to infanticide than the other, or that the State furthers any legitimate interest by banning one but not the other, is simply irrational.

Justice SCALIA, dissenting.

I am optimistic enough to believe that, one day, *Stenberg v. Carhart* will be assigned its rightful place in the history of this Court's jurisprudence beside *Korematsu* and *Dred Scott*. The method of killing a human child—one cannot even accurately say an entirely unborn human child—proscribed by this statute is so horrible that the most clinical description of it evokes a shudder of revulsion. And the Court must know (as most state legislatures banning this procedure have concluded) that demanding a "health exception"—which requires the abortionist to assure himself that, in his expert medical judgment, this method is, in the case at hand, marginally safer than others (how can one prove the contrary beyond a reasonable doubt?)—is to give live-birth abortion free rein. The notion that the Constitution of the United States, designed, among other things, "to establish Justice, insure domestic Tranquility, . . . and secure the Blessings of Liberty to ourselves and our Posterity," prohibits the States from simply banning this visibly brutal means of eliminating our half-born posterity is quite simply absurd. . . .

I have joined Justice THOMAS's dissent because I agree that today's decision is an "unprecedented expansio[n]" of our prior cases, "is not mandated" by *Casey*'s "undue burden" test, and can even be called (though this pushes me to the limit of my belief) "obviously irreconcilable with *Casey*'s explication of what its undue-burden standard requires." But I never put much stock in *Casey*'s explication of the inexplicable. In the last analysis, my judgment that *Casey* does not support today's tragic result can be traced to the fact that what I consider to be an "undue burden" is different from what the majority considers to be an "undue burden"—a conclusion that can not be demonstrated true or false by factual inquiry or legal reasoning. It is a value judgment, dependent upon how much one respects (or believes society ought to respect) the life of a partially delivered fetus, and how much one respects (or believes society ought to respect) the freedom of the woman who gave it life to kill it. . . .

While I am in an I-told-you-so mood, I must recall my bemusement, in *Casey*, at the joint opinion's expressed belief that *Roe v. Wade* had "call[ed] the contending sides of a national controversy to end their national division by accepting a common mandate rooted in the Constitution," and that the decision in *Casey* would ratify that happy truce. It seemed to me, quite to the contrary, that "*Roe* fanned into life an issue that has inflamed our national politics in general, and has obscured with its smoke the selection of Justices to this Court in particular, ever since"; and that, "by keeping us in the abortion-umpiring business, it is the perpetuation of that disruption, rather than of any Pax Roeana, that the Court's new majority decrees." Today's decision, that the Constitution of the United States prevents the prohibition of a horrible mode of abortion, will be greeted by a firestorm of criticism—as well it should. I cannot understand why those who acknowledge that, in the opening words of Justice O'CONNOR's concurrence, "[t]he issue of abortion is one of the most contentious and controversial in contemporary American society," persist in the belief that this Court, armed with neither constitutional text nor accepted tradition, can resolve that contention and controversy rather than be consumed by it. If only for the sake of its own preservation, the Court should return this matter to the people—where the Constitution, by its silence on the subject, left it—and let them decide, State by State, whether this practice should be allowed. *Casey* must be overruled.

Justice KENNEDY, with whom Chief Justice Rehnquist joins, dissenting.

For close to two decades after *Roe v. Wade*, the Court gave but slight weight to the interests of the separate States when their legislatures sought to address persisting concerns raised by the existence of a woman's right to elect an abortion in defined circumstances. When the Court reaffirmed the essential holding of *Roe*, a central premise was that the States retain a critical and legitimate role in legislating on the subject of abortion, as limited by the woman's right the Court restated and again guaranteed. *Planned Parenthood of Southeastern Pa. v. Casey*. The political processes of the State are not to be foreclosed from enacting laws to promote the life of the unborn and to ensure respect for all human life and its potential. The State's constitutional authority is a vital means for citizens to address these grave and serious issues, as they must if we are to progress in knowledge and understanding and in the attainment of some degree of consensus.

The Court's decision today, in my submission, repudiates this understanding by invalidating a statute advancing critical state interests, even though the law denies no woman the right to choose an abortion and places no undue burden upon the right. The legislation is well within the State's competence to enact. Having concluded Nebraska's law survives the scrutiny dictated by a proper understanding of *Casey*, I dissent from the judgment invalidating it. . . .

Justice THOMAS, with whom Chief Justice Rehnquist and Justice SCALIA join, dissenting.

Today's decision is so obviously irreconcilable with *Casey*'s explication of what its undue-burden standard requires, let alone the Constitution, that it should be seen for what it is, a reinstitution of the pre-*Webster* abortion-on-demand era in which the mere invocation of "abortion rights" trumps any contrary societal interest. If this statute is unconstitutional under *Casey*, then *Casey* meant nothing at all, and the Court should candidly admit it.

To reach its decision, the majority must take a series of indefensible steps. The majority must first disregard the principles that this Court follows in every context but abortion: We interpret statutes according to their plain meaning and we do not strike down statutes susceptible of a narrowing construction. The majority also must disregard the very constitutional standard it purports to employ, and then displace the considered judgment of the people of Nebraska and 29 other States. The majority's decision is lamentable, because of the result the majority reaches, the illogical steps the majority takes to reach it, and because it portends a return to an era I had thought we had at last abandoned. . . .

[Because I interpret] Nebraska's partial birth abortion statute [to] permi[t] doctors to perform D&E abortions, the question remains whether a State can constitutionally prohibit the partial birth abortion procedure without a health exception. Although the majority and Justice O'CONNOR purport to rely on the standard articulated in the *Casey* joint opinion in concluding that a State may not, they in fact disregard it entirely.

Though Justices O'CONNOR, KENNEDY, and SOUTER declined in *Casey*, on the ground of *stare decisis*, to reconsider whether abortion enjoys any constitutional protection, *Casey* professed to be, in part, a repudiation of *Roe* and its progeny. The *Casey* joint opinion expressly noted that prior case law had undervalued the State's interest in potential life, and had invalidated regulations of abortion that "in no real sense deprived women of the ultimate decision." The joint opinion repeatedly recognized the States' weighty interest in this area.

The *Casey* joint opinion therefore adopted the standard: "Only where state regulation imposes an undue burden on a woman's ability to make this decision does the power of the State reach into the heart of the liberty protected by the Due Process Clause." A regulation imposes an "undue burden" only if it "has the effect of placing a substantial obstacle in the path of a woman's choice."

There is no question that the State of Nebraska has a valid interest—one not designed to strike at the right itself—in prohibiting partial birth abortion. *Casey* itself noted that States may "express profound respect for the life of the unborn."

The next question, therefore, is whether the Nebraska statute is unconstitutional because it does not contain an exception that would allow use of the procedure whenever "necessary in appropriate medical judgment, for the preservation of the health of the mother." According to the majority, such a health exception is required here because there is a "division of opinion among some medical experts over whether D&X is generally safer [than D&E], and an absence of controlled medical studies that would help answer these medical questions." The rule set forth by the majority and Justice O'CONNOR dramatically expands on our prior abortion cases and threatens to undo any state regulation of abortion procedures.

The majority and Justice O'CONNOR suggest that their rule is dictated by a straightforward application of *Roe* and *Casey*. But that is simply not true. In *Roe* and *Casey*, the Court stated that the State may "regulate, and even proscribe, abortion except where it is necessary, in appropriate medical judgment, for the preservation of the life or health of the mother." *Casey* said that a health exception must be available if "continuing her pregnancy would constitute a threat" to the woman. Under these cases, if a State seeks to prohibit abortion, even if only temporarily or under particular circumstances, as *Casey* says that it may, the State must make an exception for cases in which the life or health of the mother is endangered by continuing the pregnancy. These cases addressed only the situation in which a woman must obtain an abortion because of some threat to her health from continued pregnancy. But *Roe* and *Casey* say nothing at all about cases in which a physician considers one prohibited method of abortion to be preferable to permissible methods. Today's majority and Justice O'CONNOR twist *Roe* and *Casey* to apply to the situation in which a woman desires—for whatever reason—an abortion and wishes to obtain the abortion by some particular method. In other words, the majority and Justice O'CONNOR fail to distinguish between cases in which health concerns require a woman to obtain an abortion and cases in which health concerns cause a woman who desires an abortion (for whatever reason) to prefer one method over another. . . .

We were reassured repeatedly in *Casey* that not all regulations of abortion are unwarranted and that the States may express profound respect for fetal life. Under *Casey*, the regulation before us today should easily pass constitutional muster. But the Court's abortion jurisprudence is a particularly virulent strain of constitutional exegesis. And so today we are told that 30 States are prohibited from banning one rarely used form of abortion that they believe to border on infanticide. It is clear that the Constitution does not compel this result.

# 12

---

# THE EQUAL PROTECTION
# OF THE LAWS

## D. NONRACIAL CLASSIFICATIONS AND THE
## EQUAL PROTECTION OF THE LAWS

### (3) Wealth, Poverty, and Illegitimacy

In *Saenz v. Roe* (1999) (excerpted below) the Court struck down California's limiting the welfare benefits of new residents to that paid by the state in which they previously resided. In doing so, Justice Stevens reaffirmed the ruling in *Shapiro v. Thompson*, 394 U.S. 618 (1969) (excerpted in Vol. 2, Ch. 12), and held that the state, in penalizing new residents, had run afoul of their constitutional right to travel. Chief Justice Rehnquist and Justice Thomas dissented.

## *Saenz v. Roe*
### 119 S.Ct. 1518 (1999)

California, which has the sixth highest welfare benefits budget in the country, amended Section 11450.03 of its Aid to Families with Dependent Children (AFDC) program in 1992 so as to limit new residents, for the first year that they live in the state, to the benefits they would have received in the state of their prior residence. Although the secretary of the Department of Health and Human Services (HHS) approved the change, which was a requirement for its going into effect, a federal district court enjoined its implementation upon finding that, under *Shapiro v. Thompson*, 394 U.S. 618 (1969) (excerpted in Vol. 2, Ch. 12), it penalized new residents and infringed on their constitutional right to travel. Subsequently, in a separate proceeding the Court of Appeals for the Ninth Circuit invalidated the

HHS's approval of Section 11450.03. However, in 1996 Congress enacted the Personal Responsibility and Work Opportunity Reconciliation Act (PRWORA), which replaced AFDC with Temporary Assistance to Needy Families (TANF). PRWORA expressly authorized any state receiving a TANF grant to pay the benefit amount of another state's TANF program to residents who lived in the state for less than one year. Whereupon, California announced that it would now enforce Section 11450.03 beginning on April 1, 1997. On that date, a class action lawsuit was filed, challenging the constitutionality of Section 11450.03's residency requirement and PRWORA's approval of that requirement. The district court found that PRWORA did not affect its earlier decision and issued a preliminary injunction against the enforcement of Section 11450.03, which the Ninth Circuit affirmed. An appeal was then made to the Supreme Court, which granted review.

The Court's decision, affirming the appellate court, was seven to two, and its opinion was delivered by Justice Stevens. Chief Justice Rehnquist and Justice Thomas each filed dissenting opinions.

Justice STEVENS delivered the opinion of the Court.

The word "travel" is not found in the text of the Constitution. Yet the "constitutional right to travel from one State to another" is firmly embedded in our jurisprudence. *United States v. Guest*, 383 U.S. 745 (1966). Indeed, as Justice STEWART reminded us in *Shapiro v. Thompson*, 394 U.S. 618 (1969), the right is so important that it is "assertable against private interference as well as governmental action—a virtually unconditional personal right, guaranteed by the Constitution to us all."

In *Shapiro*, we reviewed the constitutionality of three statutory provisions that denied welfare assistance to residents of Connecticut, the District of Columbia, and Pennsylvania, who had resided within those respective jurisdictions less than one year immediately preceding their applications for assistance. Without pausing to identify the specific source of the right, we . . . squarely held that it was "constitutionally impermissible" for a State to enact durational residency requirements for the purpose of inhibiting the migration by needy persons into the State. We further held that a classification that had the effect of imposing a penalty on the exercise of the right to travel violated the Equal Protection Clause "unless shown to be necessary to promote a compelling governmental interest," and that no such showing had been made. . . .

The "right to travel" discussed in our cases embraces at least three different components. It protects the right of a citizen of one State to enter and to leave another State, the right to be treated as a welcome visitor rather than an unfriendly alien when temporarily present in the second State, and, for those travelers who elect to become permanent residents, the right to be treated like other citizens of that State.

It was the right to go from one place to another, including the right to cross state borders while en route, that was vindicated in *Edwards v. California*, 314 U.S. 160 (1941), which invalidated a state law that impeded the free interstate passage of the indigent. We reaffirmed that right in *United States v. Guest*, 383 U.S. 745 (1966), which afforded protection to the "right to travel freely to and from the State of Georgia and to use highway facilities and other instrumentalities of interstate commerce within the State of Georgia." Given that Section 11450.03 imposed no obstacle to respondents' entry into California, we think the State is correct when it argues that the statute does not directly impair the exercise of the right to free interstate movement. For the purposes of this case, therefore, we need not identify the source of that particular right in the text of the Constitution. . . .

The second component of the right to travel is, however, expressly protected by the text of the Constitution. The first sentence of Article IV, Sec. 2, provides: "The Citizens of each State shall be entitled to all Privileges and Immunities of Citizens in the several States." Thus, by virtue of a person's state citizenship, a citizen of one State who travels in other States, intending to return home at the end of his journey, is entitled to enjoy the "Privileges and Immunities of Citizens in the several States" that he visits. This provision removes "from the citizens of each State the disabilities of alienage in the other States." *Paul v. Virginia*, 8 Wall. 168 (1869). It provides important protections for nonresidents who enter a State whether to obtain employment, *Hicklin v. Orbeck*, 437 U.S. 518 (1978), to procure medical services, *Doe v. Bolton*, 410 U.S. 179 (1973), or even to engage in commercial shrimp fishing, *Toomer v. Witsell*, 334 U.S. 385 (1948). Those protections are not "absolute," but the Clause "does bar discrimination against citizens of other States where there is no substantial reason for the discrimination beyond the mere fact that they are citizens of other States." There may be a substantial reason for requiring the nonresident to pay more than the resident for a hunting license, or to enroll in the state university, see *Vlandis v. Kline*, 412 U.S. 441 (1973), but our cases have not identified any acceptable reason for qualifying the protection afforded by the Clause for "the 'citizen of State A who ventures into State B' to settle there and establish a home." Permissible justifications for discrimination between residents and nonresidents are simply inapplicable to a nonresident's exercise of the right to move into another State and become a resident of that State.

What is at issue in this case, then, is this third aspect of the right to travel—the right of the newly arrived citizen to the same privileges and immunities enjoyed by other citizens of the same State. That right is protected not only by the new arrival's status as a state citizen, but also by her status as a citizen of the United States. That additional source of protection is plainly identified in the opening words of the Fourteenth Amendment: "All persons born or naturalized in the United States, and subject to the jurisdiction thereof, are citizens of the United States and of the State wherein they reside. No State shall make or enforce any law which shall abridge the privileges or immunities of citizens of the United States." Despite fundamentally differing views concerning the coverage of the Privileges or Immunities Clause of the Fourteenth Amendment, most notably expressed in the majority and dissenting opinions in the *Slaughter-*

*House Cases*, 16 Wall. 36 (1873), it has always been common ground that this Clause protects the third component of the right to travel. . . .

The classifications challenged in this case—and there are many—are defined entirely by (a) the period of residency in California and (b) the location of the prior residences of the disfavored class members. The favored class of beneficiaries includes all eligible California citizens who have resided there for at least one year, plus those new arrivals who last resided in another country or in a State that provides benefits at least as generous as California's. Thus, within the broad category of citizens who resided in California for less than a year, there are many who are treated like lifetime residents. And within the broad sub-category of new arrivals who are treated less favorably, there are many smaller classes whose benefit levels are determined by the law of the States from whence they came. To justify Section 11450.03, California must therefore explain not only why it is sound fiscal policy to discriminate against those who have been citizens for less than a year, but also why it is permissible to apply such a variety of rules within that class. . . .

Disavowing any desire to fence out the indigent, California has instead advanced an entirely fiscal justification for its multitiered scheme. The enforcement of Section 11450.03 will save the State approximately $10.9 million a year. The question is not whether such saving is a legitimate purpose but whether the State may accomplish that end by the discriminatory means it has chosen. An evenhanded, across-the-board reduction of about 72 cents per month for every beneficiary would produce the same result. But our negative answer to the question does not rest on the weakness of the State's purported fiscal justification. It rests on the fact that the Citizenship Clause of the Fourteenth Amendment expressly equates citizenship with residence: "That Clause does not provide for, and does not allow for, degrees of citizenship based on length of residence." It is equally clear that the Clause does not tolerate a hierarchy of 45 subclasses of similarly situated citizens based on the location of their prior residence. Thus Section 11450.03 is doubly vulnerable: Neither the duration of respondents' California residence, nor the identity of their prior States of residence, has any relevance to their need for benefits. Nor do those factors bear any relationship to the State's interest in making an equitable allocation of the funds to be distributed among its needy citizens. As in *Shapiro*, we reject any contributory rationale for the denial of benefits to new residents. . . .

The question that remains is whether congressional approval of durational residency requirements in the 1996 amendment to the Social Security Act somehow resuscitates the constitutionality of Section 11450.03. That question is readily answered, for we have consistently held that Congress may not authorize the States to violate the Fourteenth Amendment. Moreover, the protection afforded to the citizen by the Citizenship Clause of that Amendment is a limitation on the powers of the National Government as well as the States. . . .

The judgment of the Court of Appeals is affirmed.

Chief Justice REHNQUIST, with whom Justice THOMAS joins, dissenting.

The Court today breathes new life into the previously dormant Privileges or Immunities Clause of the Fourteenth Amendment—a Clause relied upon by this Court in only one other decision, *Colgate v. Harvey*, 296 U.S. 404 (1935), overruled five years later by *Madden v. Kentucky*, 309 U.S. 83 (1940). It uses this Clause to strike down what I believe is a reasonable measure falling under the head of a "good-faith residency requirement." Because I do not think any provision of the Constitution—and surely not a provision relied upon for only the second time since its enactment 130 years ago—requires this result, I dissent. . . .

In unearthing from its tomb the right to become a state citizen and to be treated equally in the new State of residence, . . . the Court ignores a State's need to assure that only persons who establish a bona fide residence receive the benefits provided to current residents of the State. . . .

States employ objective criteria such as durational residence requirements to test a new resident's resolve to remain before these new citizens can enjoy certain in-state benefits. Recognizing the practical appeal of such criteria, this Court has repeatedly sanctioned the State's use of durational residence requirements before new residents receive in-state tuition rates at state universities. *Starns v. Malkerson*, 401 U.S. 985 (1971) (upholding 1-year residence requirement for in-state tuition); *Sturgis v. Washington*, 414 U.S. 1057 (1973) (same). . . . The Court has done the same in upholding a 1-year residence requirement for eligibility to obtain a divorce in state courts, see *Sosna v. Iowa*, 419 U.S. 393 (1975), and in upholding political party registration restrictions that amounted to a durational residency requirement for voting in primary elections, see *Rosario v. Rockefeller*, 410 U.S. 752 (1973).

If States can require individuals to reside in-state for a year before exercising the right to educational benefits, the right to terminate a marriage, or the right to vote in primary elections that all other state citizens enjoy, then States may surely do the same for welfare benefits. Indeed, there is no material difference between a 1-year residence requirement applied to the level of welfare benefits given out by a State, and the same requirement applied to the level of tuition subsidies at a state university. . . .

I therefore believe that the durational residence requirement challenged here is a permissible exercise of the State's power to "assur[e] that services provided for its residents are enjoyed only by residents." . . .

(4) Alienage and Age

---

### THE DEVELOPMENT OF LAW

### Recent Rulings on Age Discrimination

| Case | Vote | Ruling |
| --- | --- | --- |
| *Kimel v. Florida Board of Regents*, 120 S.Ct. 631 (2000) | 5:4 | Writing for the Court, Justice O'Connor held that Congress exceeded its powers under |

Section 5 of the Fourteenth Amendment and violated states' sovereign immunity under the Eleventh Amendment in extending provisions of the Age Discrimination in Employment Act to state employees and ruled that state employees may not bring suits in federal courts to enforce those provisions. In reaffirming that age discrimination is not a suspect classification under the Fourteenth Amendment, Justice O'Connor emphasized that "[o]ld age also does not define a discrete and insular minority because all persons, if they live out normal life spans, will experience it." Justices Stevens, Breyer, Ginsburg, and Souter dissented.

| | | |
| --- | --- | --- |
| *Reeves v. Sanderson Plumbing Products, Inc.*, 120 S.Ct. 2097 (2000) | 9:0 | Writing for the Court, Justice O'Connor ruled that workers need not provide direct evidence that their employers |

intentionally discriminated against them in hiring and promotion decisions, in a suit brought under the Age Discrimination in Employment Act. Employees need only prove that the employer's stated reason for their dismissal was false, and juries may infer from the evidence presented whether the employer's true motive was discriminatory.

# INDEX OF CASES

Cases printed in boldface are excerpted on the page(s) printed in boldface.